PRAYING
THROUGH
THE NAMES
OF GOD

**More Books by Dr. Tony Evans and
Harvest House Publishers**

Victory in Spiritual Warfare: Outfitting Yourself for the Battle
go.tonyevans.org/victory

God's Unlikely Path to Success: How He Uses Less-Than-Perfect People
go.tonyevans.org/path

Destiny: Let God Use You Like He Made You
go.tonyevans.org/destiny

A Moment for Your Soul: Devotions to Lift You Up
go.tonyevans.org/soul

The Power of God's Names

PRAYING THROUGH THE NAMES OF GOD

TONY EVANS

HARVEST HOUSE PUBLISHERS
EUGENE, OREGON

Cover by Harvest House Publishers, Inc., Eugene, Oregon

PRAYING THROUGH THE NAMES OF GOD
Copyright © 2014 by Tony Evans
Published by Harvest House Publishers
Eugene, Oregon 97408
www.harvesthousepublishers.com

Library of Congress Cataloging-in-Publication Data
    Evans, Tony
    Praying through the names of God / Tony Evans.
        pages cm
    ISBN 978-0-7369-6051-9 (pbk.)
    ISBN 978-0-7369-6053-3 (eBook)
    ISBN 978-0-7369-7321-2 (Milano)
    1. God (Christianity—Name—Prayers and devotions. I. Title.
    BT180.N2E934 2014
    231—dc23

                                                                    2014000539

Printed in the United States of America

18 19 20 21 22 / BP-JH / 16 15 14 13 12 11

*I would like to dedicate this book to
two very special prayer warriors:
my executive assistant, Sylvia Stewart,
who intercedes on behalf of our local church,
and our receptionist, Nancy Reindl,
who prays in concert with the needs and
requests of our national ministry.*

I would like to thank my friends at
Harvest House Publishers
for their partnership in publishing.
I would also like to thank Heather Hair
for her skills and insights
in collaborating on this manuscript.

CONTENTS

INTRODUCTION

Throughout Scripture we find God's people calling on his name. Or more accurately, calling on his *names*. In the Bible, God reveals himself by various names, mostly related to his ability to meet the needs of his people. Thus, the people of God in the Bible were able to call on the name of the Lord for peace, deliverance, productivity, victory, encouragement, safety, protection, provision, power, and myriads of other things. That's true of God's people today too. Whatever our present need, God is the one who can meet that need—and he reveals himself as such by one of his many names.

Praying Through the Names of God is a tool you can use to call on the name of God for a specific need. You can do this in confidence because each of God's names in Scripture reveals an aspect of his nature suited to the need of the moment. To call on God's name in prayer is to appeal to that aspect of his character that relates to our particular need.

The Bible includes more than 85 names of God. Each one gives us a description of who God is and how he relates to his creation. We can see God's relevance to our particular situation by appealing to him based on the revelation of his names.

To help you communicate with God, I have provided a prayer related to each of his names. Prayer is heavenly permission for earthly interference. God longs to be involved with each of us on a personal level. Each of the prayers is based on the acronym ACTS:

- adoration
- confession
- thanksgiving
- supplication

You can repeat these prayers verbatim or use them to jump-start your own prayers. As you begin to pray God's name over your situation, you may find yourself continuing in prayer using your own words.

May God use this book to encourage you and help you communicate with our heavenly Father. I am excited to join you as we pray his names together.

ELOHIM

THE STRONG CREATOR GOD

*In the beginning God [Elohim] created the heavens
and the earth. The earth was formless and void, and
darkness was over the surface of the deep, and the Spirit
of God was moving over the surface of the waters.*

GENESIS 1:1-2

Adoration

Elohim, you are the strong Creator God. In you I find all of the
components of everything you have ever created. Your great imagination gave the elephant its long trunk and the leopard its spots.
By your strong arm the ocean depths were first measured and the
mountains rose. You chose what color the sky would be and how
the earth would feed itself, even bringing life through death as a
seed dies before towering into a tree. I praise you for the greatness
of your creative prowess and ingenuity. I adore you for the fullness
of your power. And I honor you for how you have made all things,
even the minutiae, work together to populate your great creation
that we call earth.

Confession

Elohim, forgive me when I fail to recognize your creative power.
Forgive me for not stopping and being awed by your hand and
the masterpiece of your creation. Forgive me for doubting where I
should trust you, even when it comes to my own life—my health

and my purpose for living. I have not always seen you in the light of your greatness, and sometimes I make you seem much smaller than you truly are. For that, I am sorry.

Thanksgiving

Elohim, thank you for the security I experience when I recognize you as the great Creator God. No one was there telling you how to make the earth rotate in its orbit so it would continually receive light and heat. And yet you did it perfectly. I thank you that you know all things and don't need me to try to figure out how to solve my issues or make my plans come about. You put the universe together with your words—thank you for knowing how to put my life together as well.

Supplication

Elohim, create great things for me to walk in. Create intersections where you merge my passion, experiences, skills, and interests together so I can fulfill the calling you have for me. Create in my heart a purity that is peaceful and appealing to those around me. Create my destiny, I pray, and then guide me into it for your name's sake and for your pleasure. I trust you to create my life's story and to give me all I need to fully live out the path you have planned for me. Thank you, *Elohim*, for being the strong Creator God.

JEHOVAH

THE RELATIONAL GOD

*This is the account of the heavens and the earth
when they were created, in the day that the LORD
[Jehovah] God made earth and heaven.*

GENESIS 2:4

Adoration

Jehovah, you are worthy of all praise and adoration. You are
the God who made the heavens and the earth. You set the stars in
their places and hung the moon where it was to remain. You rule
over all, and yet you also seek a relationship with your creation.
For that and much more, you are worthy of all praise and worship.
I lift up your name—*Jehovah*—as I seek your face. And I honor
you as you are seated on your throne above all. You are the great
and mighty God, who raises up kingdoms and subdues nations at
your choosing. In your mercy, you sustain all life and passionately
delight in our souls.

Confession

Jehovah, I come before you with a heart of contrition, knowing
I often haven't honored you as Lord and master of my life. You wait
for me to come talk to you, to wake up and greet you, or to spend
my evenings with you, but I have instead wasted time on futile
distractions. You are the relational God, who desires to walk with
me in the cool of the day, just as you walked with Adam and Eve

in those early days of your creation. Forgive me for often seeking to walk alone and ignoring the blessing and joy of your presence.

Thanksgiving

Jehovah, thank you for desiring to be close to me. Thank you for not only being high and lifted up but also dwelling with the lowly and with those who are not of a high stature. Thank you for the goodness and depth of your heart, which pours out love time and again in my life. Thank you for your grace and patience, which you lovingly manifest even in the face of my many dismissals of you. I often walk in the midst of the beauty of your creation without giving you the praise and credit you deserve. Please accept my heart of gratitude right now for all you have made and for your desire to know me fully and to empower me to know you as well.

Supplication

Jehovah, to know you and to be known by you—to experience the depth of this intimacy is my heart's greatest cry. Give me the capacity to love you deeply and to receive the love you have for me. Where my heart has become hardened or jaded, remind me of the purity of your love and gently massage it open again. Where my mind has become too analytical, give me the gift of wonder at who you are and the works of your hands. Delight my soul with your Word and with the fresh wind of your Holy Spirit. Slow my steps so that abiding with you becomes a way of life. Help me to honor you as King and to advance your kingdom.

ADONAI

MASTER OVER ALL

*O Lord [Adonai] G*OD*, You have begun to show*
Your servant Your greatness and Your strong hand;
for what god is there in heaven or on earth who
can do such works and mighty acts as Yours?

D*EUTERONOMY* 3:24

Adoration

O Lord God, my *Adonai*, you are a great and mighty God. You have opened my eyes to see your greatness and your strong hand. What god is there in heaven or on earth who can do the amazing and powerful things you can do? Who can create a mountain? Who can make the deep where the waters rest, far beyond anything we can see? Who can calm a storm with just one word? None other than you, *Adonai*. You are the Master over all. You are the Lord above all. And you are deserving of the highest honor and praise.

Confession

Adonai, I humbly bow and ask for your forgiveness for failing to honor you as I should. I ask you to show me great mercy for the many times I've gone about my day without considering that you are the Lord and Master over all. How dare I fail to acknowledge your hand? How dare I attribute to man what I ought to attribute to you? Forgive me for my shortsightedness and lack of faith.

Thanksgiving

Adonai, thank you for being my Lord and my Master and yet allowing me to know you intimately. Thank you for remembering me constantly and reminding me of your presence. Your love captivates me. Your power mesmerizes me. All I need is your love in my life, and I thank you, *Adonai*, for giving me access to you throughout my day. Any moment I need you, you are there. I love you, *Adonai*, and I thank you for granting me the privilege of loving you and receiving your love.

Supplication

Adonai, help me align my thoughts, actions, heart, decisions, and desires underneath you and your rule so I can fully experience the blessing of your hand in my life and so I can fulfill the destiny you have prepared for me. May I live out all of the days you have ordained for me, and may I discover the calling you have given me. Help me to see where I can share the knowledge of you with others and how I can spread the love you have put in my heart to those who need it the most. May your caring eyes watch over all I do. I ask you to empower me to impact the lives of those around me with your kingdom agenda.

EL BETHEL

THE GOD OF THE HOUSE OF GOD

He built an altar there, and called the place
El-bethel, because there God had revealed Himself
to him when he fled from his brother.

GENESIS 35:7

Adoration

El Bethel, I know that you can do all things and that no purpose
of yours can be thwarted. You have revealed your power and your
strength in countless ways. The heavens tell of your glory. The skies
display your marvelous craftsmanship. Day after day they continue to speak, and at night, they make you known. They speak
without a word, and their voice is silent in the skies, yet their message goes out to all of us on the earth. For since the creation of the
world, your invisible attributes—your eternal power and divine
nature—have been clearly seen, being understood through what
has been made. You have revealed yourself to all of us, *El Bethel*,
and I give you praise for who you are.

Confession

El Bethel, I confess I don't always see you when you reveal yourself to me. I don't always stand in amazement at the intricacy of
your creation. I fail to marvel at the depth of your wisdom. Forgive me for those times when you have revealed yourself to me and
yet I chose to view you with earthly eyes rather than with spiritual

discernment. Let my love abound more and more in knowledge and depth of insight so that I may be able to discern what is best and may be pure in my recognition of you.

Thanksgiving

El Bethel, thank you for making yourself known to me. Thank you for taking up residence in me through the death, burial, and resurrection of your Son, Jesus Christ, which enabled your Holy Spirit to make my spirit your house. My body is now the temple of the living God. My life is *bethel*, where you dwell, and yet I still strive to make my own decisions in spite of your desires. Thank you for your patience and longsuffering as you dwell in and with me.

Supplication

El Bethel, abide in me. Set up your home in the depths of my soul. Let your words dwell in me that I may know and live by them and for you. Reveal to me the sin I must confess and turn from so that I may be pure and blameless in your sight. Show me how to best honor you through this temple you have set up within me. Guide me in my eating habits, in my entertainment choices, and even in what I wear so that as your house—*bethel*—I may glorify you in all I do. Grant me the discernment to know how to reflect you well.

ELOHE CHASEDDI

GOD OF MERCY

My God [Elohim] in
His lovingkindness [Chaseddi] will meet me;
God will let me look triumphantly upon my foes.

Psalm 59:10

Adoration

Elohe Chaseddi, you know how I am formed. You remember
that I am dust. In your lovingkindness, you show me mercy. From
everlasting to everlasting, your love is with those who fear you, and
your righteousness with their children's children—with those who
keep your covenant. *Elohe Chaseddi*, you showed favor to your
people, and you have restored many from captivity. You have for-
given my iniquity and covered all of my sin. In your mercy, you
have withdrawn your fury and turned away from your burning
anger. Surely your salvation is near to those who fear you, that your
glory may dwell in our hearts and in our land. Your lovingkindness
and truth have met together. Righteousness and peace have kissed
each other, and for that I praise your name.

Confession

Elohe Chaseddi, I confess that sometimes I make light of your
mercy. Because of your mercy, I have been given second chance
after second chance. You have shown me forgiveness and withheld the full consequences that my actions deserve. Forgive me for

not acknowledging the power of your mercy, for not remembering what you have spared me from, and for not giving you the full devotion of my heart. Restore me, *Elohe Chaseddi*, for you have turned your indignation away from me. Revive me again that I may rejoice in you.

Thanksgiving

Elohe Chaseddi, thank you for showing me your lovingkindness. Thank you for granting me salvation not only for eternity but also in history. Thank you for speaking peace and mercy to your people—to your godly ones. Thank you for showing me mercy and empowering me to turn away from folly. I'm grateful that your truth and mercy spring from the earth and that your compassion looks down from heaven. Indeed, *Elohe Chaseddi*, you will give what is good for me, and my life will yield its produce. Mercy and peace go before you, preparing a path that I can follow.

Supplication

Elohe Chaseddi, in your mercy and compassion, you have given me great and powerful promises. You enable me to share your divine nature and escape the world's corruption and the consequences of following my fleshly desires. Your mercy equips me to live in peace, untroubled by fear of harm. Through the gift of your mercy, grant me peace of mind and heart so I will not be troubled or afraid. Your gift is from above, and it is not as the world gives. It is everlasting, and it is authentic.

EL ELOHE YISRAEL

THE MIGHTY GOD OF ISRAEL

Then he erected there an altar and called it El-Elohe-Israel.

GENESIS 33:20

Adoration

El Elohe Yisrael, you are the mighty God of Israel. Throughout history, you have chosen Israel and its people as your own. You have called them the apple of your eye (Zechariah 2:8). You have promised to make them into a great nation and to bless those who bless Israel and to curse those who curse Israel. Through Israel, you have also delivered to all of humanity the unspeakable gift of salvation through one of their own, Jesus Christ. I praise you for how you weave your plan strategically throughout time to bring about the full manifestation of your kingdom agenda on earth. I marvel at the way you have used Israel to accomplish your plan from eternity past.

Confession

El Elohe Yisrael, forgive me for failing to pray for your people, Israel, as you have instructed me to do in your Word. Forgive me for the times I have turned an uncaring heart or a blind eye to the destruction that continues to ravage them as a nation. Forgive those who bring about this destruction on the innocent people in the land, and pardon the nations who have not used their abilities to help protect or strengthen your chosen ones.

Thanksgiving

El Elohe Yisrael, I want to thank you, for you are a God of purpose and planning, and you have chosen Israel as the channel through which you have brought salvation to mankind. Through the virgin birth of Jesus Christ—Deity in human form—and his subsequent death, burial, and resurrection, you have made a way for all mankind to be free from sin, and we are all blessed. In gratitude I give you praise and thanksgiving for your plan of salvation and for delivering Israel throughout the years so that Jesus Christ could enter the world.

Supplication

El Elohe Yisrael, I ask you to grant peace to Israel. I ask you to extend your hand of compassion and mercy into the areas of destruction where men, women, and children are being injured and killed, and to rescue them. I pray for your power in the midst of chaos, your grace in the midst of despair. I lift up to you the government of Israel as well as the military and pray that your kingdom agenda will be made manifest in them. Bring the Israelite people to a saving knowledge of you, and protect them as they defend their innocent people from terrorists and militants. I bless Israel in your name today, *El Elohe Yisrael*, and ask you to bless them as well. And help me to share your heart for Israel.

EL ELOHIM JEHOVAH

THE MIGHTY ONE, GOD, THE LORD

The Mighty One, God, the LORD [El Elohim Jehovah],
the Mighty One, God, the LORD! He knows, and may
Israel itself know. If it was in rebellion, or if in an
unfaithful act against the LORD do not save us this day!

JOSHUA 22:22

Adoration

El Elohim Jehovah, you are the Mighty One! You are our mighty God, the Lord. We don't have adequate words in our language to express the great and mighty aspects of who you are. So we repeat the words in an attempt to give you a semblance of what is due you. You know all. You are over all. You are stronger than all and everything combined. I praise you for your power, strength, and might. And I humbly bow before you to honor your rightful place in my life as *El Elohim Jehovah*.

Confession

El Elohim Jehovah, pardon my iniquities, for they are many. I confess that I have not always honored you as the mighty, powerful, and strong one over all. Too often I place my own wants and desires above seeking what you want and desire in and through me. Forgive me for boxing you in, trying to figure you out, or predicting what you will do, rather than acknowledging that you are the

Lord God of gods. You know and see everything and deserve the highest place of respect in my heart.

Thanksgiving

El Elohim Jehovah, I thank you that in your great power and might, you also remain as *Jehovah*, the relational God. You are not so strong and so big that you forget to commune with someone like me. You can accomplish your plans without me, but thank you for giving me a role in your plans anyway because you love me. Thank you for your love—a healthy love, not dependent on anyone else. Because of your strength and power, you are able to love even in the face of disappointment.

Supplication

El Elohim Jehovah, teach me to love like you. Teach me to walk in your strength and might. Your Spirit lives within me, your child, and I can access your strength through your Spirit's presence. I'm not always strong, especially in the face of health crises or financial issues or difficult relationships, but you are mighty. So I ask you to intervene in my thoughts, my heart, and my mind when these situations arise so I can fully manifest your might and power in my life.

EL ELYON

THE MOST HIGH GOD

*Nebuchadnezzar then approached the opening of the
blazing furnace and shouted, "Shadrach, Meshach
and Abednego, servants of the Most High God
[El Elyon], come out! Come here!" So Shadrach,
Meshach and Abednego came out of the fire.*

DANIEL 3:26 NIV

Adoration

El Elyon, I give you praise. I praise you in your sanctuary. I praise you in your mighty expanse. I praise you for your awesome deeds, according to your excellent greatness. I praise you with music, song, and words of adoration. My soul makes its boast in you, *El Elyon*. I bless your name today, and I will forget none of your benefits. You hold the power in your hand to keep the flames of life's trials from scorching me. You have the power to save. I will not fear what man can do because you are *El Elyon*, the Most High God.

Confession

El Elyon, I see the smoke and begin to tremble when life's troubles surround me—whether in my work, my health, my finances, my family, or even in myself through anxiety, worry, or fear. Yet you are *El Elyon*, and you know when even a hair falls from my head. You protected Shadrach, Meshach, and Abednego when they were tossed to their certain death. But that sentence of death became the promise of life as you intervened. Forgive me, *El Elyon*, for looking only at what I can see, things that seem so certain to harm me physically or emotionally, rather than looking at you.

Thanksgiving

El Elyon, receive my heart of gratitude for being the Most High God. Accept my spirit of gratefulness for holding my world together in the palm of your hand. You are patient, kind, and gentle, yet you are also powerful, mighty, and strong. Thank you for showing me time and again that you are over all, and for delivering me from the snares of the enemy.

Supplication

El Elyon, I ask you to manifest your powerful might within me more and more each day. Too often I look to myself when I get into a difficult situation. Like Shadrach, Meshach, and Abednego, I see the flames. But so often I become fearful. Help me instead to look to you, the everlasting God, the Creator of the ends of the earth. You are not only the Creator God, you are *Elyon*, Most High. You do not faint or grow weary. Your understanding is unsearchable. Give me power when I feel faint, and increase my strength when I am weak. Help me to wait well on you as the young Hebrews did in the midst of the roaring flames.

EL EMUNAH

THE FAITHFUL GOD

Know therefore that the LORD your God is God;
he is the faithful God [El Emunah], keeping his
covenant of love to a thousand generations of those
who love him and keep his commandments.

DEUTERONOMY 7:9 NIV

Adoration

El Emunah, your faithfulness convinces me that nothing can
ever separate me from your love. Neither death nor life, neither
fear nor worry—not even the powers of hell can separate me from
you because you are faithful. I honor and adore you for the faithfulness you show me even when I am unfaithful to you. I praise
you for keeping your covenant of love not only to me but also to a
thousand generations of those who love you and seek you with all
of their hearts, minds, and souls. I praise you, *El Emunah*, for the
faithfulness that you revealed in writing and recording your Word
for my instruction so that through endurance and the encouragement of your Scriptures, I might have hope.

Confession

El Emunah, your faithfulness reminds me that I'm not always
faithful to you. Although I have a heart to be faithful to you, situations arise that evoke fears and doubt, tempting me to make
choices of self-preservation, selfishness, and greed. I confess that

I am not always *emunah* to you or to those around me. I have dropped the ball far too often. Forgive me for my frailty and emotional exploits. Remind me again and again of your faithfulness so that I will grow to be more like you.

Thanksgiving

El Emunah, thank you for your faithfulness to me. Thank you for the many times I've seen you show up in my life when I didn't know how I was going to pay the bills, how I would ever be healed, or how I would find relational peace in the midst of chaos and conflict. Thank you for being faithful time and time again to the words you have placed in my heart and to your promises in Scripture.

Supplication

El Emunah, it's easy to begin to doubt your faithfulness when I have to keep coming back to you again and again to confess where I've blown it. I ask you to strengthen the resolve in my spirit to truly believe that you are *El Emunah* and that because you're faithful, you will never abandon me. You have promised never to leave me or to forsake me. I ask you to open the eyes of my heart so I can see your faithfulness and stand without a shadow of a doubt in the confidence of a covenant relationship with you.

ELOHEI TEHILLATI

GOD OF MY PRAISE

O God of my praise [Elohei Tehillati],
Do not be silent!

PSALM 109:1

Adoration

Elohei Tehillati, you are my strength and my song. I extol you because you have become my salvation. I give you praise because you are the one true God. Who is like you among the gods? Who is like you in all of the earth? Who is majestic in holiness, awesome in praises, and continually working wonders? Only you, *Elohei Tehillati*. You are deserving of my praise and my adoration. Great are you, God, and greatly to be praised. You are to be feared above all else. I ascribe to you the glory due your name and come before you in humble prayer to worship you, O *Elohei Tehillati*.

Confession

Elohei Tehillati, I bow before the majesty of your glory and all that is due to you, and I confess I'm guilty of trying to take your praise and steal your glory. Too often I attempt to take credit for that which you have done. I fail to remember that you are the one who shows favor, opens doors, and gives me the opportunities I experience in my life. I can do nothing apart from you, so you are worthy of all of my heartfelt and truest praise.

Thanksgiving

Elohei Tehillati, I give you thanks and praise your holy name. You are good, and your lovingkindness endures forever. I will give thanks to you according to your righteousness and your grace. I praise your name of praise, *Elohei Tehillati*. Let the words from my mouth and the meditation of my heart bring you delight rather than anguish. Guide me into a lifestyle of gratitude and praise. Thank you for doing that in the days ahead.

Supplication

Elohei Tehillati, fill me to overflowing with gratitude. Give me eyes to see you all around me. Open up my mind to spiritual things. Help me to discern spiritual truths so I can stand amazed at who you are. Refine my soul so that praise becomes my natural response rather than something I'm prompted to do at church. Keep me from subtle sins that distract me from glorifying and honoring you. Set my heart free so that I might receive the fullness of your presence and power in my life.

EL HAKABODH

GOD OF GLORY

The voice of the LORD is over the waters;
the God of glory [El Hakabodh] thunders,
the LORD thunders over the mighty waters.

PSALM 29:3 NIV

Adoration

El Hakabodh, you have revealed your glory in Jesus. He is the radiance of *El Hakabodh* and the exact representation of your nature. Because of Jesus, I am able to come into your presence with unveiled face and behold the glory of the Lord. I praise you and adore you—transform me into your image from one degree of glory to another. Your glory is so magnificent that heaven needs no sun or moon to shine on it, for you, *El Hakabodh*, give it light, and the lamp is the Lamb of God, Jesus Christ.

Confession

El Hakabodh, you are a jealous God who will not share your glory with others. Forgive me for turning my eyes to humanity, thinking that this person or that person delivered me from a particular trial. Rather, it was you who used them to bring about your intended deliverance. Forgive my shortsightedness in not always seeing your glory through your creation, your works, your Word, and your Spirit.

Thanksgiving

El Hakabodh, you are light, and in you is no darkness at all. Thank you for your permeating glory and for sustaining this world and everything in it. Without your glory, sin would overtake and destroy all life and hope. Thank you that in Jesus Christ your glory became flesh and dwelt among us, giving us an opportunity to see the glory of the only Son from the Father, full of grace and truth.

Supplication

El Hakabodh, your voice is over the waters, and your glory thunders throughout the land. Whom shall I fear but you? I ask you to intervene on my behalf when enemies seek to bring me down. Your glory is strong and mighty, like thunder and lightning. You see all my enemies and will protect me from them. Keep me from getting in the way of your glory by being prideful, trusting in my own strength, or seeking revenge. As you delivered Joseph from the pit—not only once, but twice—deliver me, *El Hakabodh*, from the ill will of those who oppose me and stand against your truth.

ELOHIM CHAYIM

THE LIVING GOD

This is how you will know that the living God [Elohim Chayim] is among you and that he will certainly drive out before you the Canaanites, Hittites, Hivites, Perizzites, Girgashites, Amorites and Jebusites.

JOSHUA 3:10 NIV

Adoration

Elohim Chayim, you are the living God. I lift up your name in praise and exaltation, for you are deserving of my highest adoration. In you is life. All that is living finds its existence from you. Without you, we have no life. Every animal, cell, flower, human being—every living thing receives its life from your own. Awesome and great *Elohim Chayim*, I praise your powerful, life-giving name.

Confession

Elohim Chayim, you are the source of my life. Every breath I take, each morning that I wake—these are from you, the living God. Your life extends into mine, giving me the opportunity to experience your creation. Forgive me for the times I don't seem to value the life you have given to me. Forgive me for making poor eating choices or not sleeping as much as I should. Forgive me for not treasuring and taking care of the gift of life you have given to me. You are the living God, and you are intimately involved in all that I do.

Thanksgiving

Elohim Chayim, thank you for being active and engaged in my everyday life. You are not a God who sits far off, removed and distant, having no say in what happens to me. Just as you drove out the Canaanites, Hittites, Hivites, Perizzites, Girgashites, Amorites, and Jebusites from before the Israelites, you are alive and moving in the situations of my life as well. Thank you for your interest, care, concern, and loving participation in me, through me, and around me.

Supplication

Elohim Chayim, reveal your ways to me. Show me your path. Walk beside me, before me, pointing the way. O living God, guide me and direct me. Make me aware of your presence when I am not. Give me discernment to see your work behind the scenes when I do not see your hand. And please go before me, as you did with the Israelites, to drive out my enemies and help me to settle into the destiny you have for me.

EL HAYYAY

THE GOD OF MY LIFE

By day the LORD directs his love,
at night his song is with me—
a prayer to the God of my life [El Hayyay].

PSALM 42:8 NIV

Adoration

El Hayyay, by day you direct your love, and at night your song is with me. You are the God of my life. You direct my steps according to your will and desire. You cause me to walk on firm footing. When it is dark, you light the way and give comfort. At times I cannot see the beauty stretching out before me because my eyes are dulled by darkness. But in those times, you ask me to have faith in you, to cling to your Word that when the sun rises, I will see the greatness of your goodness in my life.

Confession

El Hayyay, you know that I have questioned more than I should have. I have asked to see the end when I don't trust the means you are using in my life. I have doubted your heart when I couldn't see your hand or when your ways seemed confusing. Forgive me for not resting in your name, *El Hayyay*, the God of my life, and for trying to be in charge of my life myself. Pardon my impetuous spirit.

Thanksgiving

El Hayyay, I thank you for truly being the God of my life. You know me better than anyone else could ever know me. What's more, you are authentic in your care. You have no hidden motives for uncovering who I am, so I thank you for your love—so real, so kind, so deep. Thank you, *El Hayyay*, for guiding me and directing my steps. Thank you for speaking to me when I seek you and your way. Thank you for being *El Hayyay*.

Supplication

El Hayyay, the God of my life, be very close to me. Open my ears to hear you. Soften my heart to discern your Spirit. Help my eyes to recognize when you are weaving something new in my life. Turn my frustration and anger away from people who seem to be obstacles in my life, *El Hayyay*, and help me to remember you are sovereign. Nothing happens to me that doesn't first pass through your hands. Kings see you and bow down. I pray that each moment I will honor you and live in that same spirit of humility before the God who knows what steps I should take and who guides me.

ELOHIM KEDOSHIM

THE HOLY GOD

*Joshua said to the people, "You are not able to serve the
LORD. He is a holy God [Elohim Kedoshim]; he is a jealous
God. He will not forgive your rebellion and your sins."*

JOSHUA 24:19 NIV

Adoration

Elohim Kedoshim, there is none like you, none holy like the
Lord. There is no one beside you—no one is even close to you. I
praise you as the Lord my God, and I consecrate myself before you
to be holy as you are holy. I lift up your name, for you are the one
who is high and lifted up and who lives within eternity and is called
Elohim Kedoshim. You dwell in a high and holy place, yet you also
dwell with those who are contrite and of a humble heart. In your
holiness, you revive the lowly and comfort the hurting.

Confession

Elohim Kedoshim, I know that you want me to be holy as you
are holy, and I seek that with all my heart. But I also know I have
fallen short in the past, I fall short of it in the present, and will fall
short of it in the future. In my finiteness I sin far too often. My
sins of commission and sins of omission offend your beauty and
purity. Forgive me for the worry, doubt, fear, anxiety, anger, and
even lack of love in my heart at times. Cleanse me in your holiness.

Thanksgiving

Elohim Kedoshim, thank you for being completely pure and true. I thank you, the Holy One, that you made a way through your Son, Jesus Christ, to allow me into your presence. Even though you are holy, you desire my heart and want to share an intimate relationship with me. Your holiness is the beauty I see in this world, and I thank you for blessing me and blessing the earth by reflecting your holiness in your creation.

Supplication

Elohim Kedoshim, I ask you for your patience. I ask you to continue to show me favor and patience as I strive each day to be more of a reflection of you than I have been in the past. I know the lack of pure holiness in my spirit saddens you, and yet you still love me. Make my heart holy like yours. Speak to me before I make wrong choices or as I'm thinking wrong thoughts. You know how to speak to me in a way that I can hear, so please intervene in my life and empower me to live in holiness day in and day out.

EL KANNA

THE JEALOUS GOD

*You shall not bow down to them or worship them; for
I, the LORD your God, am a jealous God [El Kanna],
punishing the children for the sin of the parents to the
third and fourth generation of those who hate me.*

EXODUS 20:5 NIV

Adoration

El Kanna, you are a jealous God. I give you praise because of the
restraint you have shown in my life each time I place something
higher than you. Sometimes I look to another person to solve my
problem or provide what I think I need rather than looking to
you, but I know that your character as *El Kanna* feels dismissed or
hurt. Yet your love as my Savior brings me mercy time and time
again. I adore you, for you are strong, *El Kanna*, yet you also show
me grace and favor.

Confession

El Kanna, you know how many times I've gone to a friend
before seeking your presence or wisdom in a situation. You know
how often I try to bail myself out of trials or temptations rather
than looking to you. Your favor and your hand have protected me,
opening doors for me and granting me success, and yet I feel pride
in what I misconstrue to be my own doing. Forgive me for pro-
voking your jealousy, *El Kanna*. Forgive my insensitivity and sin.

Thanksgiving

El Kanna, thank you for promising in your Word that you will punish the children for the sin of the parents to the third and fourth generation of those who hate you. Yet you have sent your Son, Jesus Christ, to offer mercy and to break the cycle of your wrath whenever a heart turns toward you. Thank you for being a jealous God, because that indicates the depth of your care. If you didn't love me deeply—more deeply than I can even understand— you would not be jealous. What I did or did not do would not matter to you. Your jealousy assures me of your care.

Supplication

El Kanna, I ask you to teach me ways to honor you in my life, in my actions, in my words, and in my thoughts. Let my lips be sprinkled with that which brings you delight. Let my desires reflect your own yearnings. Enable me to always give you the praise that is due you. Give me spiritual discernment to recognize your hand at work, and empower me with the boldness to proclaim your goodness to others. I ask for your favor, *El Kanna*, that I might live a life that truly respects you and blesses others.

ELOHEI MA'UZZI

THE GOD OF MY STRENGTH

God [Elohei] is my strong [Ma'uzzi] fortress;
And He sets the blameless in His way.

2 SAMUEL 22:33

Adoration

Elohei Ma'uzzi, you are my strong fortress. You are the God of my strength. In you I find all that I need. In you are power, might, and force. I praise you for your mighty hand. I lift up your name to give you honor because of your greatness. Your creation testifies to your power. The mountains rise to proclaim your strong arm. The ocean depths reveal your force. The moon keeps its place because of your great strength. The sun flames as a result of your own creative prowess. You are to be held in the highest esteem, and I praise you, *Elohei Ma'uzzi*.

Confession

Elohei Ma'uzzi, forgive me for doubting your strength and failing to access it in my own life on a regular basis. As a child of the King, I have access to your strength, and yet I often try to walk in my own limited power. Surely you must sometimes wonder why I don't rely on your strength, *Elohei Ma'uzzi*. Forgive me, Lord, for neglecting such a great gift.

Thanksgiving

Elohei Ma'uzzi, I thank you for being strong and powerful—and for being strong for *me*. You are a personal God who desires to see me live out my destiny according to your calling and the purpose for which you have created me. In order to do this, I need your strength. I don't have to juggle everything in my life on my own because you have told me that if I come to you, you will give me rest. Your yoke is easy and your burden is light because you bear them for me. Thank you, *Elohei Ma'uzzi*, that in you I find my strength.

Supplication

Elohei Ma'uzzi, gird me with your great strength. Make my heart strong and my mind wise. Give me strength to withstand temptation whether the temptation is to gossip, to use my time unwisely, or to harbor bitterness. Whatever it is, give me strength—let *your* strength be mine. Strengthen my hands to do all you have assigned me to do. Strengthen my mind to think big because I serve a big God. Strengthen my resolve when life seems unfair or a struggle. *Elohei Ma'uzzi*, forever be my strength.

ELOHIM MACHASE LANU

GOD OUR REFUGE

Trust in him at all times, you people;
pour out your hearts to him,
for God [Elohim] is our refuge [Machase Lanu].

PSALM 62:8 NIV

Adoration

Elohim Machase Lanu, you are my refuge. I praise you because
you are trustworthy. I praise you for keeping my heart safe with
you. I adore you because you provide a place where I can go when
the storms of life toss me here and there. Some people brag about
the things they own, and they look to their own hands for their
protection. Other people boast in their abilities or their wit to
keep them safe. Yet I boast in your name, *Elohim Machase Lanu*,
because in you I will rise and stand upright despite what life sends
me. You are my refuge.

Confession

Elohim Machase Lanu, I don't always run to you when I should.
Particularly when I feel vulnerable, I turn instead to things I can
see to help me, or I turn to things that will distract me rather than
going where I know I am safe—and that is to you. You are my
strong tower, my refuge. Forgive me for not always acknowledging or taking advantage of all that you are and all that you want to
be in my life.

Thanksgiving

Elohim Machase Lanu, thank you for your power. Thank you for your strength. Thank you for being a refuge to me and to those who seek you. Thank you for caring about each one of us—your children—with such tenderness. Thank you for shielding us as we face life's troubles and for going through them with us. As Jesus stood on the hill overlooking the city, tears came to his eyes because his people had not turned to him as their King and their refuge. I thank you for such vulnerability—you are a great and mighty God, yet you care so gently for your people. Truly, you are my *Elohim Machase Lanu*.

Supplication

Elohim Machase Lanu, I pray that you will stand guard in my life and guide me away from trials and tribulations that put me in perilous situations. But you have warned us that in this life we will face trials and tribulations, so I know I will sometimes be in great need. I ask, *Elohim Machase Lanu*, that you will do something in those times to get my attention, to remind me to look to you. Keep me from faltering on my own—from trying to comfort and protect myself, and from looking to someone other than you to be my refuge.

ELI MAELEKHI

GOD MY KING

They have seen Your procession, O God,
The procession of my God, my King [Eli
Maelekhi], into the sanctuary.

PSALM 68:24

Adoration

Eli Maelekhi, you are God, my King. I worship you, for you are seated on your mighty throne. I lift up your name and give you praise. Your kingdom rules over all. Your kingdom agenda is to advance your rule—the visible manifestation of your comprehensive rule over everything. You sit high and lifted up, enthroned above everyone and everything. You are King. I humbly bow before you to offer you my praise, honor, and adoration.

Confession

Eli Maelekhi, I ask for your pardon and forgiveness for not always giving you the honor due to you as King. Please forgive me for the many times I've pressed my own agenda rather than advancing your kingdom agenda. Grant me mercy, *Eli Maelekhi*, for seeking to reign where you should rightly reign and for turning to my own ways rather than to yours. Forgive me for not using your Word as a guide in every decision I make.

Thanksgiving

Eli Maelekhi, I come before you with thanksgiving and extol you with praise. You are the great King above all kings and the great God above all gods. I enter your courts with thanksgiving and come into your presence with a heart of gratitude. Thank you for choosing me as an heir to your kingdom, for making me a child of the King. By virtue of my relationship with you through your Son, Jesus Christ, I am entitled to all the spiritual blessings you have for me in your kingdom. Thank you for your abundant favor.

Supplication

Eli Maelekhi, I ask you to give me a kingdom mindset. Help me to advance your kingdom agenda on earth. Give me wisdom to understand what it really means to pray "thy kingdom come" and "thy will be done." Help me turn off distractions that take me away from time that rightly belongs to you, my *Eli Maelekhi*, my King. May I be fully equipped to serve you and your kingdom in the way you desire and deserve. Show me the spoils of your kingdom, and share with me the beauty of your provision.

HUIOS TOU THEOU

THE SON OF GOD

*Simon Peter answered, "You are the Christ, the
Son [Huios] of the living God [Theou]."*

MATTHEW 16:16

Adoration

Huios tou Theou, you are the Christ, the Son of the living God.
I worship you, for you have come to take away the sins of the
world. After God the Father spoke long ago through the prophets,
he then chose to speak to us through you, *Huios tou Theou*, whom
he has made heir of all things. It is also through you that he made
the world. You are the radiance of God's glory and the exact representation of him in every way. I lift up your name, for you have sat
down at the right hand of the Majesty on high, having inherited a
more excellent name than any other.

Confession

Huios tou Theou, I confess my sins before you and ask for your
forgiveness. Because of your death, burial, and resurrection, I am
able to receive forgiveness for all I have done wrong. I ask for your
great mercy as your blood cleanses me from all unrighteousness.

Thanksgiving

Huios tou Theou, thank you for the majesty of your name. No
other name is as great as yours. Thank you for humbling yourself

and entering the earth as a babe in a manger. More than that, thank you for humbling yourself to the point of death so that I might receive fellowship with your Father in heaven. Thank you for the kindness of your love and the power of your name. In your name, demons have been cast out. In your name, I find protection, peace, and power. I thank you, *Huios tou Theou*, for your presence in my life.

Supplication

Huios tou Theou, I ask you to help me honor you with my life. Help me to keep you close to me in all I do. I understand that as I abide in you and your love, your will and your way will abide in me. Whatever I ask the Father in your name will be given when it aligns with your will. Please enable me to walk closely with you and to keep your words hidden in my heart. My desire is to please you in all I do, and I pray you will guide me down the path you have ordained for me.

EL NEKAMOTH

THE GOD WHO AVENGES

He is the God who avenges [El Nekamoth] me,
who subdues nations under me.

PSALM 18:47 NIV

Adoration

El Nekamoth, you are the God who avenges me, who subdues my enemies under me. You tell me in your Word that vengeance is yours, and this is because you are *El Nekamoth*. You know how to prepare a table before me in the presence of those who oppose me. You set me in high places when others try to take me down. I praise you because you are the God of justice. It is a terrible thing to fall in the hands of *El Nekamoth*. I glorify your name because you have shown yourself to be all-powerful in my life.

Confession

El Nekamoth, I admit that I rush to seek my own vengeance when I feel I have been wronged. I confess to you that I like to see swift retaliation, and when I don't see you intervening, I sometimes try to avenge myself. Please forgive me for not being silent when others oppose me. Forgive me for not leaving vengeance to you. Forgive me for wrapping my own agenda into life's situations when I should leave the matter in your hands.

Thanksgiving

El Nekamoth, thank you for being the God who avenges. Thank you for balancing the scales when I stay out of the equation. Thank you for your heart of justice. Thank you for your compassion, which seeks to right wrongs when I've been treated unfairly. When someone has unjustly accused me or sought to remove my influence or bring me pain, you see, you hear, you care...you are there. You are *El Nekamoth*—you avenge me, and for that I am truly grateful.

Supplication

El Nekamoth, I ask you to give me restraint so that I don't seek my own revenge and then miss out on witnessing your intervention on my behalf. Help me not to harbor bitterness or unrighteous anger toward those who have sought harm against me and thereby prohibit you from carrying out what you wish on my behalf. Where I have been unfairly treated, *El Nekamoth*, please remove, correct, or bring to repentance the person or persons who have done it.

EL NOSE

THE GOD WHO FORGIVES

LORD our God,
you answered them;
you were to Israel a forgiving God [El Nose],
though you punished their misdeeds.

PSALM 99:8 NIV

Adoration

El Nose, you are to Israel a forgiving God. Though they faced the consequences of their actions, you did not hold a grudge or bear anger against them. You let them learn from their wrong choices, but you also let them learn the depth of your forgiveness. You are high and worthy of all praise, *El Nose*, because the expanse of your love covers my sins. You love me enough to teach me through the results of my wrong choices, but you are also there as *El Nose* to love me when I turn to you and ask for forgiveness.

Confession

El Nose, I experience this name of yours afresh on a daily and often hourly basis. When you forgive me, I experience your pure love. I can't even count all the things I must confess. Some of my failures are seemingly benign, as when I doubt your steadfastness or sovereignty. Others are more serious, as when I speak unkindly to another person, whom you love. But you know all of my sins. I beg for your mercy, and I'm grateful to receive it, *El Nose*.

Thanksgiving

El Nose, my heart overflows with gratitude to you for your capacity to forgive. Words can't adequately express the thankfulness within me for this, your greatest gift. If I had to be perfect to obtain your favor, your blessings, or the daily sustenance you provide, I wouldn't last a day. But because of your name, *El Nose*, and the character it reflects, I can receive your awesome gifts and kindnesses. Thank you for the grace and mercy of your forgiveness in my life and all it allows me to experience.

Supplication

El Nose, I ask you to help me to not take lightly the gift of your forgiveness. Create in me a heart of gratitude that will motivate me to serve you with my life. Remind me of the terrible price you paid—the sacrifice of Jesus Christ—to offer me forgiveness. There is no condemnation for me because I am in Christ Jesus. I pray that I will truly own and walk in this truth. Write it on my mind, heart, and soul, and help me stand confidently before you, approaching your throne of grace boldly.

ELOHENU OLAM

EVERLASTING GOD

For this God is our God for ever and ever [Elohenu Olam];
he will be our guide even to the end.

PSALM 48:14 NIV

Adoration

Elohenu Olam, you are my God forever and ever. You will be my guide even to the end. In you there is no beginning and there is no end. I am never afraid that you will abandon me by leaving me unexpectedly. Neither will you cease to exist. I know you now, and I will know you in eternity, and even more so, for then I will see you face-to-face. You are worthy of all praise and adoration. You are worthy of my highest honor and deepest respect. You do not sit in time, but you are outside of time, inviting me to join you in the drama of the ages unending. How vast are your thoughts, stretching beyond what any mind could comprehend. You know all things, and in you life itself will never end.

Confession

Elohenu Olam, I confess that I can hardly grasp what my life may be like in five years, or ten. To comprehend a God who exists before time and will experience no end is beyond my capabilities. Forgive me for not fully appreciating your power, intellect, and character. The universe is merely a pebble in your hand, and yet I get so consumed by what I hear on the news or see at the workplace or experience in my relationships. A God who is *Elohenu Olam* is not easily overwhelmed because you see it all. You know how it began and you know how each situation will end. You will always be there as the everlasting God. Forgive me for worrying rather than trusting in your wisdom and power.

Thanksgiving

Elohenu Olam, thank you for the magnificence of your expanse. Thank you for inviting me to know you, for spending moments with me and making them wonderful…special…filled with your presence. Everlasting God—*Elohenu Olam*—you are not bound by time, so my heart overflows with gratitude because you stoop to be with me in time.

Supplication

Elohenu Olam, what can I ask the everlasting God? You know best what I need and when I need it. You see the end before the beginning, and you know the path I am to take. I ask for wisdom, for you are the great and wise everlasting God. I ask for the ability to slow down and focus my thoughts on you in my daily life. Place yourself on my mind when I wake up each morning, that I might start my day right. Remind me of who you are so I don't waste the time you have given me. Help me to use my time to advance your kingdom for your glory, for the good of others, and for the fulfillment of my destiny.

ELOHIM OZER LI

GOD MY HELP

Surely God is my help [Elohim Ozer Li];
the Lord is the one who sustains me.

PSALM 54:4 NIV

Adoration

Elohim Ozer Li, you are the God who helps me and sustains me. When I am in need, you are there. When I am alone, you are near. When I don't know my way, you guide me or come alongside me to walk with me as I find it. You are worthy of praise, *Elohim Ozer Li*, because your great arm reaches out to help those in need. You provide me with all I need to carry out the purpose for which you have placed me on earth. You sustain me with the kindness of your love, the wisdom of your mind, and the strength of your arm. I adore you, *Elohim Ozer Li*, with all that is within me.

Confession

Elohim Ozer Li, please pardon me for the fears I entertain when I don't know how to get through a trial or a struggle. Fear wells up in me as a natural emotion, but I confess I don't quickly chase it away with the truth of your character or with the truth of your Word as I should. Please have mercy on me for not expecting your help but rather having to be reminded that you are truly there.

Thanksgiving

Elohim Ozer Li, thank you for your goodness to me and for your help, which is from beginning to end. You don't take a vacation from my life. You don't rest when I'm sleeping. You don't leave me to my own devices, but you are there when I call on you for help. And even when I don't call on you, out of your great mercy and compassion you help me then as well. Thank you for your goodness and the greatness you offer me through the blessing of your help and sustaining power.

Supplication

Elohim Ozer Li, I ask for your help. Many things are weighing me down, but you know the one most pressing issue facing me today, and I ask you to intervene. Please guard me from responding to this situation inappropriately. Guard me from turning to my own ways and human wisdom. Show me your hand as a reminder that you are near and that you are my sustaining help. Do help me this very day, *Elohim Ozer Li*, for I depend on you in every way.

EL ROI

THE GOD WHO SEES ME

*[Hagar] gave this name to the LORD who spoke to
her: "You are the God who sees me [El Roi]," for she
said, "I have now seen the One who sees me."*

GENESIS 16:13 NIV

Adoration

El Roi, through this great name, you reveal your heart in a
uniquely powerful way. In this name, you remind us that you see
us as individuals. You see, and thus you know. When you saw
Abraham on the mountaintop and witnessed his trust in you, you
provided a ram as *Jehovah Jireh*. Likewise, as *El Roi* you see where I
am, and you respond. Because you see me, I know that I am truly
known. To be known by you—to not be forgotten—is one of
my greatest needs, so this name comforts me greatly. I praise you
because you are not a distant God who sits far off, isolated from
those you have made. Instead, you see me, you are with me, and
you care.

Confession

El Roi, when I feel alone and forgotten, please forgive me for
neglecting to acknowledge your name. Forgive me for grumbling
when I don't see the one who sees me. Help me to remember that
you are there. Yes, you are the God who sees me in whatever situation I'm facing. Pardon me for failing to see the God who sees me.

Thanksgiving

El Roi, when Hagar sat alone and afraid in the desert, you made yourself known to her as the God who sees. Thank you for making yourself known to me, too, as the God who sees. Whatever trial I face, you see it. Whatever opposition rises up against me, you see it. Whatever health issue comes upon me, you see it. Thank you for your attentiveness to me and for your willingness to reveal yourself as the God who sees.

Supplication

El Roi, you *see*. I ask you to act on my behalf when you see me wronged unfairly. I ask you to defend and vindicate me when you see me accused unjustly. When others toil less and yet receive more reward, I ask you to see the diligence and tenacity of my heart and open doors for me that only you can open—because you see. You do not see me as humanity does. You do not judge by external appearances or by what the world esteems. You see my heart, and I pray now what Nehemiah prayed so long ago: "Remember me with favor."

EL SALI

GOD MY ROCK

The LORD lives, and blessed be my rock;
And exalted be God, the rock [El Sali] of my salvation.

2 SAMUEL 22:47

Adoration

El Sali, I bless your name. You reign over all. You stand strong and tower high like a mountain of rock jutting up from the earth's surface. You are not swayed or moved when storms come. Upon the strength of who you are, I find a firm foundation to build my life. You provide my salvation and the stability of my times.

Confession

El Sali, again and again I enter into my day with the greatest of intentions, ready to trust in you as your names remind me of your great power. Yet when the winds blow and the waves crash against the shore, I forget to look at you, my *El Sali*. I forget that you are strong and that you have not been moved by what moves me. Forgive me each and every time I have not sought refuge in you, *El Sali*.

Thanksgiving

El Sali, you deserve my gratitude. You stay steady when all else around me crumbles and falls. Thank you for your power and strength. Thank you for being my rock, the God of my salvation.

Thank you for Jesus Christ and his sacrifice for my sins. Thank you for not only saving me for eternity but also for offering me salvation while on earth. Accept my humble words and heart of prayer as I bow before you to thank you for all you have done for me.

Supplication

El Sali, as my rock and my salvation, be my stability when things are not stable. Whisper to me in those times when I no longer see you there. When our national economy falters and so much around me seems to be on unsteady ground, help me focus on your never-ending kingdom and eternal throne. They are unshakable because you are *El Sali*, my solid rock.

EL SHADDAI

ALMIGHTY GOD

When Abram was ninety-nine years old, the LORD appeared to him and said, "I am God Almighty [El Shaddai]; walk before me faithfully and be blameless. Then I will make my covenant between me and you and will greatly increase your numbers."

GENESIS 17:1-2 NIV

Adoration

El Shaddai, you are great and mighty in power. Your understanding and wisdom know no limits. Your might knows no bounds. As the heavens are higher than the earth, so your ways reach higher than my own. You surround me with the blessings of your provision as you covenant with me through your Son, Jesus Christ. The balancing of the clouds and the wondrous works of the earth are nothing compared to you, who sit enthroned in might and valor.

Confession

El Shaddai, look upon me with a caring heart and witness the many struggles I face. Have compassion, for you see me seeking to follow you—and often failing to do it well. Forgive me when I'm unfaithful to you, for you have asked me to walk before you faithfully. Forgive me when blame is due me, for you have asked me to be blameless. Let Christ's blood cover me in your covenant as I seek your blessing, *El Shaddai*.

Thanksgiving

El Shaddai, thank you for the promises you gave to Abraham. Thank you for communing with him and establishing the Abrahamic covenant, through which you have truly blessed all the nations on the earth. Thank you for your faithful love, which you promised to Abraham on that day and have also promised to me through your beloved Son, Jesus Christ.

Supplication

El Shaddai, show me how to honor you with my faith, just as Abraham did throughout his life. I want to be a person of great faith and to experience you as *El Shaddai* in my life. At times, Abraham didn't exhibit the faith that he displayed in his later years, and in so doing, he delayed your covenant with him. Help me to not cause delays in my destiny but rather to walk upright in faith starting even from today. Strengthen the muscles of my heart and my soul so I am willing to risk everything for you. Help me to demonstrate my dedication and commitment to you, my King, and to your kingdom agenda on earth.

ELOHIM SHOPHTIM BA-ARETS

THE GOD WHO JUDGES IN THE EARTH

Then people will say,
"Surely the righteous still are rewarded;
surely there is a God who judges the earth
[Elohim Shophtim Ba-arets]."

PSALM 58:11 NIV

Adoration

Elohim Shophtim Ba-arets, when justice is done, the righteous rejoice. Those who have sought to obey you are filled with delight. Your justice is like the spring rain, bringing blessing and life to those it touches. Let justice roll down like the waters, like an ever-flowing stream. Yet while your justice brings happiness to the righteous, terror engulfs the evildoers. It is a terrifying thing to fall into the hands of the living God. Yet for the righteous you wait to be gracious, and you exalt yourself to show mercy. You are a God of justice who judges the earth, and blessed are all those who wait for you.

Confession

Elohim Shophtim Ba-arets, you judge both the righteous and the wicked. You love justice and have promised not to forsake your saints. I confess that I don't always fall into the category of the righteous, for I have often done things that are offensive to you, things for which I am not proud. Have mercy on me as I wait patiently and expectantly for your mercy.

Thanksgiving

Elohim Shophtim Ba-arets, thank you for using just scales and for rewarding those who diligently seek you. As I witness the chaos and turmoil in our world today—terrorist attacks, random acts of violence, or any number of things—I know you sit as the God who judges the earth. There will be a time of accounting for those who bring evil on the lives of the innocent, and I'm grateful that you are ultimately in control.

Supplication

Elohim Shophtim Ba-arets, so much happens in the world today—both righteous and evil. I ask you to rain down your blessing on the many who are seeking to bring about healing to the suffering on earth. Reward their righteousness with your favor. I also ask you to intervene against the evil in the land that would cause disruption and disunity. As you have done in the past in wars and battles, confuse the enemy of peace and goodness on every front and strengthen those who defend life, liberty, and freedom.

EL SIMCHATH GILI

GOD MY EXCEEDING JOY

Then I will go to the altar of God,
To God, my exceeding joy [El Simchath Gili];
And upon the lyre I shall praise You, O God, my God.

PSALM 43:4

Adoration

El Simchath Gili, yours is the greatness, power, glory, victory, and majesty. All that is in heaven and on earth belongs to you. Because of this and more, you are my exceeding joy. You are my delight, and I come before you in prayer to exalt your name forever. I praise your glorious name, for in your hand are both power and might, and it is by your word that you make great or bring down. There is none higher than you and none more worthy of all of my praise.

Confession

El Simchath Gili, all things come from you and are created by you. Even my joy and my delight are from your blessed hand. Forgive me for seeking joy in other sources than you. Pardon me for turning to things outside of you to seek what can be found only in you. You are the source of my joy.

Thanksgiving

El Simchath Gili, thank you for your beauty and the delight you took in making your creation. You have placed me in the midst of a wondrous and amazing world. You astound me with your creatures and with your imagination. The depth of your knowledge is limitless, and because of it I find joy in learning and discovering new things. Thank you for the pleasures I'm blessed to experience as a result of knowing and loving you.

Supplication

El Simchath Gili, show me your wonders. Delight me with that which delights you. When I witness the things that make your heart glad, mine becomes glad as well. Give me the pleasure of knowing you intimately because in you I will find my joy and my delight. Help me also to bring joy to other people I come into contact with. Give me a sweet spirit radiating your love and pleasure to those around me. Help me to say kind and encouraging words and to always think on things that are pure.

ELOHIM TSEBAOTH

GOD OF HOSTS

*O God of hosts [Elohim Tsebaoth], restore us
And cause Your face to shine upon us, and we will be saved.*

PSALM 80:7

Adoration

Elohim Tsebaoth, you are the great God of hosts, the commander of armies. Who is a king like you, full of glory and might, whose voice instructs those in battle on behalf of your children? You are a king both strong and mighty, fierce in battle. Lift up your heads, all you gates and all you ancient doors—lift up and see that the King of glory is here. The God of hosts is this King—he is the commander of all and worthy of my highest praise.

Confession

Elohim Tsebaoth, you are great and powerful. Kings see you and bow down. Armies tremble in your presence and respond to your call. Yet I often dismiss you as if you were not present. I go about my business with little or no regard for how my thoughts or actions impact you and your kingdom. Forgive me for my lack of honor and respect to you, for you are worthy of all praise.

Thanksgiving

Elohim Tsebaoth, thank you for securing my salvation. When you make your face shine on me, I experience all I need to gain every victory. Because of you and what you have already accomplished for me at Calvary, I don't fight for victory—I fight *from* victory. The battle has already been won for me by the God of hosts, who defeated Satan and disarmed him, making a mockery of him when Christ rose from the dead. Thank you for being the strong and mighty commander of the armies of angels.

Supplication

Elohim Tsebaoth, will you fight my battles for me? When I'm struggling to overcome an emotional issue, will you give me the victory? Or when someone is treating me unfairly, will you intervene? With you on my side, I will always come out victorious. I have nothing to fear when I recognize and acknowledge you as *Elohim Tsebaoth*. David defeated Goliath with only one stone—it doesn't take much to win a battle when you lead the charge. Give me the faith and the skill of David to be a valiant warrior under you and to defeat the enemy's attempts to divert me from your purposes.

ELOHE TISHUATHI

GOD OF MY SALVATION

Deliver me from bloodguiltiness, O God,
the God of my salvation [Elohe Tishuathi];
Then my tongue will joyfully sing of your righteousness.

PSALM 51:14

Adoration

Elohe Tishuathi, deliver me from the guilt in my life, for you are God, my Savior. I give you praise and adoration because of your powerful hand and your heart to forgive me of my sins. Your righteousness has been transferred to me through the death, burial, and resurrection of your Son, Jesus Christ, and his sacrifice for my sins on the cross. You have imputed his righteousness to me through your salvation. I honor you and lift you up, for you have surely delivered me from all my enemies.

Confession

Elohe Tishuathi, I come before you with my head bowed low and my heart saddened by the sins I have committed against you. They are many, and you know each one. You even know the ones that are unknown to me. I confess to you that my heart is sometimes hardened, sometimes faithless, often questioning you. I confess a lack of love—pure love—toward those who oppose me, irritate me, or don't show me kindness. I confess I have turned away from many in need even though you have blessed me so that

I might be a blessing to others. Selfishness is alive in me, and I ask for your forgiveness for that and for all my sins.

Thanksgiving

Elohe Tishuathi, thank you for your greatest gift, which is salvation. Thank you for offering me forgiveness time and time again, for showing me how to live with grace and mercy. You have every right to judge me, punish me, and neglect to use me to advance your kingdom, and yet you continually seek a relationship with me in so many ways. You desire my worship, and yet I can worship only because you have brought me salvation. You have done so much for me, and my heart overflows with gratitude and humility before you.

Supplication

Elohe Tishuathi, I do not take lightly the sacrifice you made for my salvation so that your righteousness could be imputed to me through Jesus Christ. Help me understand how great this salvation truly is so that I will live each day in continual gratitude, motivated to serve you all the more. Help others to come to know you as Lord and Savior. Open their hearts and minds to receive you as *Elohe Tishuathi*. Send into this world those who will tell of your great love and testify to the saving power of your Son, Jesus Christ. Visit people in sermons, teachings, books, and even dreams so they also may be saved.

ELOHE TSADEKI

GOD OF MY RIGHTEOUSNESS

Answer me when I call,
O God of my righteousness [Elohe Tsadeki]!
You have relieved me in my distress;
Be gracious to me and hear my prayer.

PSALM 4:1

Adoration

Elohe Tsadeki, you are my righteous God. From you flow mercy, grace, might, and strength. In you exists all I need to live in abundant joy. Your righteousness brings about the beauty we see in one another—the acts of kindness, the moments of intimacy and pure love. None of these are possible apart from you because goodness and righteousness stem from the core of who you are. I would not know love if it were not for you, so I praise you and honor you for who you truly are.

Confession

Elohe Tsadeki, I confess my unrighteousness to you and acknowledge the guilt of my sin. Where I have wronged others, forgive me. Where I have failed to promote you as King, Lord, and Savior, have mercy on me. Where I have chosen my own desires over yours, grant compassion and guidance to show me the better way. Forgive the pain I have caused others, and help them to forgive me as well. Help me to mend my broken relationships. Make me a vessel of your righteousness, grace, and peace.

Thanksgiving

Elohe Tsadeki, thank you for the beauty of your righteousness. Thank you for the power of your righteousness. Thank you for the mercy you hold in tandem with your righteousness. I'm grateful for your righteousness, which leads me in the path that I should follow. As I walk through valleys and trials, your righteousness guides me. Our nation is stumbling due to greed, irresponsibility, and other sins, and we need your righteousness in our hearts to restore us. Thank you for making your righteousness and wisdom available to all through your Spirit and your Word.

Supplication

Elohe Tsadeki, I pray today especially for our communities and our nation. We are in great need of knowing this name of yours once again. Your righteousness gave us the might and power we experienced in the past. Because you are *Elohe Tsadeki*, we have enjoyed the fruit that comes from following you. Yet now our communities and our nation have abandoned you. We have removed your name in so many places. Pour your righteousness into the hearts of our leaders and into the hearts of our citizens that we may rise up once again and reclaim the greatness you alone allowed us to experience. Give us relief from the violence, poverty, and strife we face in our land.

ELOHE YAKOB

THE GOD OF JACOB

May the LORD answer you when you are in distress;
may the name of the God of Jacob [Elohe Yakob] protect you.

PSALM 20:1 NIV

Adoration

Elohe Yakob, you are the great and mighty God. And yet you are also a personal God who identifies with mere humans, like Jacob. I praise you because you are awesome and because you are able to answer my prayers and the prayers of all who seek you. In the early centuries of history, you attached yourself to the Israelite people as their God, the *Elohe Yakob*. Yet through Jesus Christ you are my God, and you have often blessed the land where I live because of your goodness. I honor you for honoring those who seek and serve you.

Confession

Elohe Yakob, forgive me for failing to recognize your personal attachments in my own life. As you are the God of Jacob, you are also the God of me. Through Christ I am reconciled to you and have been given every spiritual blessing in the heavenly places. You will even have a new name for me when I one day enter your presence in eternity. Forgive me for being too tied to the things I can see, smell, and touch rather than to you, the great God of Jacob and the great God of me.

Thanksgiving

Elohe Yakob, thank you for hearing me in my distress and for delivering me time and time again. Your name is a name of protection. Thank you for demonstrating that protection throughout history. You hid the spies in Jericho by leading them to a woman named Rahab. You gave the Israelites entry into the Promised Land by stopping up the waters of the Jordan when it would have been too high to cross. Yours is a name of protection and provision, and I thank you for revealing this to me in so many ways.

Supplication

Elohe Yakob, I ask that the personal name you have given to Jacob, you will give to me. You called and chose Jacob to be your servant. But through Jesus Christ, you have also called and chosen me to understand your kingdom agenda and to advance your glory on earth. Deliver me from my distresses. Show me the paths where I can cross waters that are too deep for me to cross on my own. Hide me in the recesses of your palm. Grant me favor where I go that I might fully walk in the promises and the blessings you have assigned for me.

ELOHEI MAROM

GOD ON HIGH

With what shall I come to the LORD
And bow myself before the God on high [Elohei Marom]?
Shall I come to Him with burnt offerings,
With yearling calves?

MICAH 6:6

Adoration

Elohei Marom, you sit high and lifted up, seated on your throne. You are the King who reigns over all. Seraphim fly around you, each having six wings. With two wings they cover their faces, with two wings they cover their feet, and with two wings they fly, shouting to one another, "Holy, holy, holy is the God on high" as the foundation of the temple trembles at your very presence. You are to be honored, loved, and adored at all times.

Confession

Elohei Marom, touch my lips with a burning coal as an angel touched the lips of Isaiah as he stood in your presence. For I am also a person of unclean lips, I live among a people of unclean lips, and my eyes have seen the King, *Elohei Marom.* Humbly I bow before you and ask for your cleansing power in my life. I confess I have not recognized your glory for all its worth or acknowledged your greatness in the expanse of your creation. The oceans are but a drop of water to you. The galaxies like gnats in space. The highest peak on earth is merely a footstool for you because you are God on high, *Elohei Marom.*

Thanksgiving

Elohei Marom, thank you for the vastness of who you are. Thank you for allowing me to experience the breadth of your creation the way you have. My body alone is a majestic piece of intricate art and science woven together by the Master Creator. Thank you for holding all things together. *Elohei Marom*, I lift up my grateful spirit for all you have made and for all you are.

Supplication

Elohei Marom, show me your grandeur. Bring me into your courts with praise, with humility, and with awe. Send me as you sent Isaiah when he saw you high and lifted up, seated on your throne, to do your will at your bidding, to advance your kingdom on earth. The kings of earth are nothing compared to you. The problems we face in our homes, churches, and communities, and the challenges we see in our nation and world—they are easily solved by a God who is high and exalted. Grant wisdom to me and to others so we can live according to your will.

ELOHEI HAELOHIM

THE GOD OF GODS

For the LORD *your God is the God of gods [Elohei Haelohim]*
and the Lord of lords, the great, the mighty, and the awesome
God who does not show partiality nor take a bribe.

DEUTERONOMY 10:17

Adoration

Elohei Haelohim, you are the God of gods and the Lord of lords.
You are the great and powerful all-knowing God. No one can force
your hand. You do not bend to special-interest groups or to pres-
sure from people. You rule according to righteousness and truth.
You show no partiality, but have made a way for all to come into
a relationship with you through the sacrifice of your Son, Jesus
Christ. I praise you and lift up your name, *Elohei Haelohim*, the
God of gods, Lord of lords, and King of kings.

Confession

Elohei Haelohim, how blessed are those who trust in you! You
make their paths straight and guide them into the way everlasting.
You are closer than a brother and more faithful than a spouse. You
are also higher than any other—you are the God of gods. Forgive
me for looking to idols—those things I look to in place of you—
when I am in need or facing a trial. Forgive me for making my
career an idol, or my status, or even my relationships. Have mercy
upon me, *Elohei Haelohim*, and draw me close to you.

Thanksgiving

Elohei Haelohim, accept my gratitude for all you are and all you do. Thank you for this day, for waking me up this morning, and for giving me another moment in life. Thank you for surrounding me with the people in my life—some to sharpen me, some to comfort me, and others to reflect your closeness to us, your creation. Thank you for the majesty of your handiwork—for dotting the landscape with your brilliant pieces of art. *Elohei Haelohim*, I owe all my gratitude to you because everything I enjoy and everything that helps me grow ultimately comes from you.

Supplication

Elohei Haelohim, reign and rule over the difficult circumstances of my life that seek to defeat me. You are stronger than all, higher than all, and wiser than all—you are *Elohei Haelohim*, and nothing is impossible with you. My issues and my trials are nothing to you. You can solve them with just a thought or an inclination. Please let me see you supremely represented in my everyday life. Plant your thoughts in my mind so that your kingdom will advance on this earth.

EHYEH ASHER EHYEH

THE ETERNAL, ALL-SUFFICIENT GOD

> God said to Moses, "I AM WHO I AM" [Ehyeh
> Asher Ehyeh]; and He said, "Thus you shall say to
> the sons of Israel, 'I AM has sent me to you.'"
>
> EXODUS 3:14

Adoration

Ehyeh Asher Ehyeh, there is so much power in your name. There is peace in knowing your name. You are all-sufficient in your name. By your name you control the outcome of nations. You led the Israelites into freedom by assuring them that you are all-sufficient. How can I lift up your name in adoration when it is already so high? I am feeble in my attempts to praise you, for you deserve the praise of all of creation and for all eternity. Yet you still accept my praise and desire it and sit enthroned upon it, O *Ehyeh Asher Ehyeh*.

Confession

Ehyeh Asher Ehyeh, you hold the world in your hands. You do not exist in time, but are before time and will be after time. I confess to you the finiteness of my mind. I confess my insufficiency in light of your all-sufficiency. Pardon the impatience I feel when something goes wrong at work, or at home, or in a relationship. Forgive my bitterness, my resentment, and my doubts that you are good, great, mighty, fair, and just.

Thanksgiving

Ehyeh Asher Ehyeh, thank you for showing me the same love that you showed to Moses at the burning bush. Thank you that your love is with me not only in my crises but also in my quiet days. Thank you for choosing me to be your friend even though you are so much greater than anything that has ever existed or ever will exist. Your sufficiency makes me whole. Thank you for knowing me fully and giving me a heart to know you and pray to you.

Supplication

Ehyeh Asher Ehyeh, what can I ask a God who is the great I AM? I can't even understand you—you are beyond my capacity of thinking or comprehending. If I ask according to my own thoughts, I will surely limit all that you can do and all that you desire to do in me and through me. Your will is what I want, although I do not know how to discern it on my own. But I trust you, and so I pray that your Spirit will graciously pray into my life the things that you want me to accomplish and experience. Empower me to cooperate with you as you continue to manifest your kingdom on this earth.

JEHOVAH ADON KOL HA-ARETS

THE LORD, THE LORD OF ALL THE EARTH

As soon as the priests who carry the ark of the
LORD—the Lord of all the earth [Jehovah Adon Kol
Ha-arets]—set foot in the Jordan, its waters flowing
downstream will be cut off and stand up in a heap.

JOSHUA 3:13 NIV

Adoration

Jehovah Adon Kol Ha-arets, as the Israelites sought to enter the Promised Land, a river blocked their way. They had seen you part the Red Sea, but now it was time to see you in a new way. You told them you had given them the land and that you would drive out their enemies if they would do what you said. So you sent their priests into the Jordan, and as their feet touched the water's edge, you stopped the waters from flowing and dried up the riverbed so the people could cross over, offering you honor and praises all along the way. You are a great and awesome God who still does mighty acts on behalf of your people.

Confession

Jehovah Adon Kol Ha-arets, sometimes it can be difficult to see how you will make a way where there seems to be no way. I wish I could know what the Israelites were thinking as they stood along the banks of the Jordan after hearing that you had instructed them to walk through it into the Promised Land. Did they doubt you, just as I sometimes do? Did they immediately give you thanks, or did they wait until they saw the water begin to stop flowing? I confess to you, *Jehovah Adon Kol Ha-arets*, I often forget that you have control over the earth you created. The elements are nothing to you—after all, you made them. You are not bound by the laws of science. The earth is your playground, and it is under your command.

Thanksgiving

Jehovah Adon Kol Ha-arets, thank you for your creation and for your creative prowess. It's comforting to know that nothing is too big for you or removed from your control. The winds may rage and the storms shake the ground, but nothing shakes you. Nothing surprises you. Thank you for your ability to subdue the creation underneath you. In you I find my peace.

Supplication

Jehovah Adon Kol Ha-arets, I ask you for special grace that I might keep my eyes on Jesus Christ—not on the waves surrounding me, and not on the water you're calling me to walk out onto. Even if the waters were peaceful, my mind would still doubt that I could walk on them. As Peter sank when he looked down, I ask that I will not sink—may my eyes always be on you. And as the Israelites witnessed you stop the running water, I pray that you will help me to do whatever you ask me to do so that I can witness your miraculous interventions in my life.

JEHOVAH CHEREB

THE LORD, THE SWORD

Blessed are you, Israel!
Who is like you,
a people saved by the LORD [Jehovah]?
He is your shield and helper
and your glorious sword [Chereb].
Your enemies will cower before you,
and you will tread on their heights.

DEUTERONOMY 33:29 NIV

Adoration

Jehovah Chereb, I give you my all because in you I find my all. You are my shield. You are my helper. You are my glorious sword. Those who rise up against me cannot stand in your presence. Simply trusting in you brings about the deliverance I seek. Aligning my life under your commands gives me your covenantal covering. You tread on the heights of all. Nothing is too large for you to overcome. My trials and my troubles are as nothing in your hand—you easily remove them.

Confession

Jehovah Chereb, make your powerful presence known to me so I will call on you and not lean on my own understanding when I face a new battle. Too often I take the fight into my own hands. I try to win against a foe stronger than me. You are my glorious sword, and in you alone I find my victory. Pardon my iniquity for carrying the chains you have already removed, for being bound by that from which you have already released me.

Thanksgiving

Jehovah Chereb, thank you for your holy power. Thank you for your mighty sword. Thank you for giving me victory over anything I face. No battle is too tough for you to win. No addiction is too strong for you to break. No sin is too great for you to forgive. Great is your faithfulness. Great is your might. Thank you for the faithfulness you show as you fight against those who seek to bring down your people. You are the great and mighty sword—the one who is over all.

Supplication

Jehovah Chereb, may I find the peace that comes from trusting in this name. You have my back, and nothing can overcome me if I but trust in you. Therefore I will delight in freedom and rest in you. I want to enter into the rest you promise to those who seek you. As I know your names, and as I live in the abiding truth of who you are rather than solving my own problems and righting my own wrongs, I will prevail. I appeal to you today to make your names alive in my mind—cause me to remember them just at the right time—so that I will live in the power of your great names.

JEHOVAH TSABA

THE LORD OF HOSTS

*David said to the Philistine, "You come to me with a
sword, a spear, and a javelin, but I come to you in the
name of the LORD of hosts [Jehovah Tsaba], the God
of the armies of Israel, whom you have taunted."*

1 SAMUEL 17:45

Adoration

Jehovah Tsaba, your name alone was able to give David the confidence to approach a trained warrior nearly twice his size. Because
of the power of your name, David didn't hesitate to approach his
enemy and defeat him. I give you honor and praise and full adoration, for you are worthy of all glory. You have the power to defeat
the greatest and largest of opponents because you are *Jehovah Tsaba*,
the Lord of hosts, the God of the armies of Israel.

Confession

Jehovah Tsaba, King Saul tried to weigh David down with hundreds of pounds of armor because the king looked at the size of
the enemy and saw sudden death. The Israelite soldiers were so
afraid, they refused to go out and face him themselves. It's easy
to criticize them for not having the bravery of young David, but
I admit I sometimes shrink back from opposition that seems to
loom large over me. Forgive my cowardice in the face of trouble,
Jehovah Tsaba, for it is an affront to your power and sovereignty.

Thanksgiving

Jehovah Tsaba, my enemies may come at me with a sword, a spear, and a javelin, but I thank you for being greater still. I may be attacked by every side, but I thank you for surrounding all and being over all. Thank you for the power of your name, which gives me the courage and the confidence to stand in the face of what would normally frighten me. Because of you I can boldly proclaim, as David did, that I come in the name of the Lord of hosts.

Supplication

Jehovah Tsaba, go before me as I enter into battle. Just as you taught David to trust you when he killed the bear and the lion, help me to see where and how you're preparing me for the battles I will one day face. When I reach those battles, remind me that I have already overcome in other situations and that just as you were with me then, you are with me now. Give me the courage of David to refuse the armor people try to give to me and instead to take up the armor of your name. In that power, I can overcome anything.

JEHOVAH GIBBOR MILCHAMAH

THE LORD MIGHTY IN BATTLE

Who is the King of glory?
The LORD strong and mighty,
The LORD mighty in battle [Jehovah Gibbor Milchamah].

PSALM 24:8

Adoration

Jehovah Gibbor Milchamah, today I join with Moses, who praised and adored you as the Lord mighty in battle.

> The LORD is my strength and song, and He has become my salvation, this is my God, and I will praise Him; my father's God and I will extol Him. The LORD is a warrior; the LORD is His name. Pharaoh's chariots and his army He has cast into the sea; and the choicest of his officers are drowned in the Red Sea. The deeps cover them; they went down into the depths like a stone. Your right hand, O LORD, is majestic in power, Your right hand, O LORD, shatters the enemy. And in the greatness of Your excellence You overthrow those who rise up against You (Exodus 15:2-7).

Confession

Jehovah Gibbor Milchamah, forgive me for taking my battles into my own hands and my own intellect, trying to scheme my way into victory rather than trusting in you, the great, powerful, and mighty warrior. Forgive my attempts at righting wrongs, oftentimes only contributing to more wrongs as I seek to overcome in my own strength.

Thanksgiving

Jehovah Gibbor Milchamah, thank you for being mighty in battle and for being faithful to send forth your burning anger against unrighteousness when your people rise up and call on your name in humility. I need not fear anyone or anything when the greatest of warriors guides me, and I give you thanks for revealing this truth to me today.

Supplication

Jehovah Gibbor Milchamah, be my strength and my song so that I might offer you praise each day. Visit me in my distress and overcome those who oppose me. When people spread untruths about me, close their lips—just as you closed the jaws of the lions when Daniel was tossed into the den. Let me walk through each day in peace, knowing that if I will be still before you, you will fight on my behalf. Help me to live in purity and trust so that I dare not stay your hand with my own unrighteousness. In quietness and trust will I find my escape from all that troubles me. Grant me the grace of both virtues this day and every day. Then I will lift up your name in my heart in total praise and awestruck wonder.

JEHOVAH MAGINNENU

THE LORD OUR DEFENSE

Our shield [Maginnenu] belongs to the LORD [Jehovah],
And our king to the Holy One of Israel.

PSALM 89:18

Adoration

Jehovah Maginnenu, my shield belongs to you because you are my defense. You are all-powerful, all-knowing, and ever ready to stand in defense of those who fear you and put their trust in you. At the blast of your breath you are able to separate waters, as you did for the Israelites when they crossed the Red Sea. With your powerful voice you are able to still the storm, as you did on the Sea of Galilee. All matter succumbs to your command, and nothing that pursues me—whether it has to do with my finances, health, work, or relationships—can overtake me when I trust in you as my defense.

Confession

Jehovah Maginnenu, I often say that you are my defense, but when my back is up against the wall, I quickly look for someone or something else to bail me out. When my emotions are untested and calm, I acclaim your virtues all day long. Yet when faced with trials and tribulations, I tend to jump ship and try to swim for shore rather than trust your power to save me. Forgive me for forgetting so easily that you truly are my defense, and forgive me for seeking to justify and vindicate myself rather than allowing you to do so.

Thanksgiving

Jehovah Maginnenu, thank you for your ready defense. Thank you for always being on the alert. Thank you for not sitting far away and making yourself unreachable to me. As our military is sent to retaliate against terrorism directed at innocent people's lives, you also rise up when I am unfairly treated. Your very presence assures me of your love, and I am grateful for the times when you have vindicated me publicly.

Supplication

Jehovah Maginnenu, when I'm falsely accused by someone out of jealousy, resentment, or any other reason, I pray you will quickly reveal the lie behind the accusation and silence those who seek to do me harm. I seek your kingdom and the advancement of your will on earth, and I pray you will keep at bay those who try to dissuade me from living a life of fruitfulness for you. Be my defense against Satan, the father of lies, not only in my own mind by reminding me of your truth, but also when others believe the twisted lies he tries to spread about me.

JEHOVAH GOELEKH

THE LORD YOUR REDEEMER

You will drink the milk of nations
and be nursed at royal breasts.
Then you will know that I, the LORD [Jehovah],
am your Savior,
your Redeemer [Goelekh], the Mighty One of Jacob.

ISAIAH 60:16 NIV

Adoration

Jehovah Goelekh, I know that my Redeemer lives and that you
have sent redemption to me, your child, through your Son, Jesus
Christ. You have ordained your covenant, and all of your purposes
will stand. You formed me for a purpose, and you have called me
by my name—great and holy is your name. You are the God who
works wonders, and by your power, you redeem people to yourself. You are the first and the last—there is no other God besides
you. None of those who take refuge in you will be lost. I praise you
because you have redeemed me and delivered me time and time
again from the hand of the enemy.

Confession

Jehovah Goelekh, forgive me for taking your redemption too
lightly and not living in the light of that truth. I confess my lack of
understanding of all the dangers you have rescued me from. Were
my eyes to be completely open as they will be one day, I would

know the full extent of your redemption. Or if you were to give me insight, just as you gave to Elisha's servant when he saw the armies of your angels ready and able to defend them against the king of Aram, I would give you the praise you truly deserve. Forgive my lack of total comprehension of how you redeem me each day.

Thanksgiving

Jehovah Goelekh, thank you for the many ways you have stood guard around me. You have protected me from unseen dangers and redirected me as you did Balaam with his donkey and the angel. You are always working things out behind the scenes, and I'm grateful that despite my lack of awareness and acknowledgment, you still redeem me day after day—my health, my relationships, my career...so many things. You sustain me with the finest nourishment of all—your grace. I'm grateful for your daily mercies and blessings, which come to me by way of your redeeming strength.

Supplication

Jehovah Goelekh, be my constant Redeemer and my ever-present help in trouble. Redeem me from myself—my sinful propensities, wasteful indulgences, and doubt. Give me the grace of the greatest virtues and mold me into the person you have purposed me to be. I ask that I will drink the milk of nations as you have said. Grant me fruitfulness and abundant blessing according to your perfect will, for the advancement of your kingdom, and for the good of others. Use me as a vessel of redemption to those in need.

JEHOVAH ELOHIM

LORD GOD

This is the account of the heavens and the earth
when they were created, in the day that the LORD
God [Jehovah Elohim] made earth and heaven.

GENESIS 2:4

Adoration

Jehovah Elohim, in the account of the heavens and the earth
when they were created, you are featured prominently as the Creator. From your creative mind came the concept. From your loving heart came the reality. From your mouth came the words that
spoke the earth and the universe into existence. I stand on ground
that you have spoken into being. I breathe air that you determined
would enter my lungs and give life to the cells in my body. I honor
and adore you for your creative power and genius, Lord. You are
worthy of all my praise.

Confession

Jehovah Elohim, I confess I don't fully understand or grasp the
true magnitude of all you have made. Everything is perfectly created so that we all live in a natural cycle that sustains itself and pro-
duces life. But you are also intimately involved in your creation.
You are not only *Elohim* but also *Jehovah*. Forgive me for failing
to honor you at the highest level due you. Forgive me for neglecting to show you the respect you deserve. Pardon my heart when it

selfishly seeks to take credit for something you have created and planted in my own life—such as my skills, gifts, and talents, *Jehovah Elohim*.

Thanksgiving

Jehovah Elohim, thank you. Thank you for all you have created. Thank you for being mindful to put beauty in the midst of your creation. Thank you for being mindful to give me the ability to appreciate and enjoy what your hands have made. Every day is a gift from you. You send the rain to water the ground and restore life where it has become dry. You tell the stars where to hang in the sky and call the tide when it is time to rise. Thank you for the magnificence of who you are and for allowing me to glimpse even a fraction of that magnificence through your creation.

Supplication

Jehovah Elohim, the majesty you have displayed in your creation reminds me that you are all-powerful. The details you have given to each species on earth reminds me how much you intimately care. You have created me as a relational being, and I desire to connect with your other children, *Jehovah Elohim*. Show me how to best glorify you as I love others because of my love for you. And open up my heart to receive love from others as a reflection of your love for me. I ask you to display your creative powers in me. Bring my gifts and treasures to full fruition according to the purpose for which you have given them to me.

JEHOVAH ELOHIM AB

THE LORD GOD OF YOUR FOREFATHERS

So Joshua said to the sons of Israel, "How long will you put off entering to take possession of the land which the LORD, the God of your fathers [Jehovah Elohim Ab], has given you?"

JOSHUA 18:3

Adoration

Jehovah Elohim Ab, you are the Lord God of my forefathers. You were present before time began and have walked with my ancestors and all who have come before me. You are the one who spoke to Moses at the burning bush. You gave Joshua instructions on how to defeat Jericho. *Jehovah Elohim Ab,* you were with Mary when she gave birth to the Messiah and laid him in a manger. You are the same today and tomorrow as you were yesterday. I praise you for keeping a record of your connection with humanity through the Bible, and for preserving this record to share with me. I have a lot to learn from your interactions with my forefathers, *Jehovah Elohim Ab,* and I honor you for giving me the opportunity and the desire to know more.

Confession

Jehovah Elohim Ab, Lord God of my forefathers, I confess I don't always make a connection between what you have done in the past and what you are doing currently in my life. I neglect to study your Word and learn your character through the way you interacted with those who came before me. I am a child of Abraham and an heir to the covenants you have established with my spiritual forefathers. Yet I confess my lack of understanding of what that entails and of my birthright. What I do not know, I cannot ask for. Forgive me for not taking full advantage of what you have established already through your relationship with my spiritual forefathers.

Thanksgiving

Jehovah Elohim Ab, thank you for going before me and paving the way for the destiny you have called me to walk in. Thank you for teaching me through the way you've worked with others. Thank you for my birthright as a kingdom citizen and your child. You have given me every spiritual blessing in the heavenly places already, and now—as so many of my forefathers did—I just need to access them. Thank you for choosing this time for me to do just that and for giving me wisdom through your relationship with those who came before me in your Word.

Supplication

Jehovah Elohim Ab, I ask for wisdom and understanding, which are yours to give to me. Open my eyes to fully appreciate what my spiritual forefathers have left to me through the ministry of their lives. As you were to them, *Jehovah Elohim Ab*, be also to me. I want to be like Moses, Joshua, and Mary in my faith and in your power.

JEHOVAH EL ELYON

LORD GOD MOST HIGH

*Abram said to the king of Sodom, "I have
sworn to the LORD God Most High [Jehovah
El Elyon], possessor of heaven and earth."*

GENESIS 14:22

Adoration

Jehovah El Elyon, you are the Lord God Most High. I praise you
for your exalted position. I honor you, for you are seated above
all else. I lift up your name and bless who you are—the possessor
of heaven and earth. You are the friend of humanity. You are the
highest being in existence. For all of this and more, I lift you up as
King. Manifest your kingdom rule on earth as you demonstrate
your power and might above all.

Confession

Jehovah El Elyon, I confess I sometimes place myself mentally
in your position. I like to call the shots in my own life. I want
to make my own decisions. I forget that you are the Lord God
Most High and choose instead to pretend that I am. Forgive me
when I fail to recognize you in your rightful place and honor you
as the Lord God Most High. Forgive me when I don't trust that
you know what's best and what will advance your kingdom in the
long run. Forgive my audacity in making choices apart from your
divine perspective.

Thanksgiving

Jehovah El Elyon, I thank you for being not only the Most High God but also the Lord. You do not rule simply to rule. You have a reason for what you do. Thank you for dwelling in my life and heart and inviting me into the drama of your kingdom. Thank you that I can pray directly to you, the God who is above all and over all.

Supplication

Jehovah El Elyon, I ask you to show me how to live my life in a way that will advance your will, passion, and agenda on earth. Through Christ, you taught us to pray, "Your kingdom come, your will be done." I seek your hand in my life so my words and actions will manifest the kingdom of the Lord God Most High on earth. And when I face difficulties and trials, help me to remember that you are Lord over all and that you care. You've got my back if I will simply trust you. Show me this truth again and again as I look to you to meet my every need.

JEHOVAH EL EMETH

LORD GOD OF TRUTH

Into Your hand I commit my spirit;
You have ransomed me, O LORD, God
of truth [Jehovah El Emeth].

PSALM 31:5

Adoration

Jehovah El Emeth, I lift up your name in praise and adoration. You are the Lord God of truth. You are the presence and essence of truth. Truth originates from you, and we are incapable of discerning truth without you. I honor you for your clarity and your wisdom, for the understanding and application of truth. I bless your name, *Jehovah El Emeth*. Let all the nations find wisdom in you. Let all the communities find restoration in your ways. Let all the churches recognize the power of your truth and teach truth always. And let each individual praise you for the purity of your truth.

Confession

Jehovah El Emeth, I bow before you and ask you to forgive me for twisting your truth. Sometimes I add my perspective in an attempt to change your truth. I don't always let your truth run through my thoughts but rather choose to worry, doubt, or listen to my own perspective over yours. Your Word is truth, yet I have neglected to memorize the promises in your Word in order to always hide them in my heart and thoughts. Have mercy on me for seeking to undermine your truth with worldly wisdom.

Thanksgiving

Jehovah El Emeth, thank you for the truth, which is perfectly pure. Thank you for the truth, which brings no confusion. Truth is your viewpoint on a matter—thank you for not hiding your truth or making it difficult for me to grasp. Your truth is readily available to me in your Word. Thank you for giving me the ability to read, *Jehovah El Emeth*, and for empowering me to discern your truth from what the world tries to paint as truth but is actually a lie from the devil. Thank you for the power of your truth, which makes life's choices easier when aligned under your truth.

Supplication

Jehovah El Emeth, my desire is to live according to your truth, and yet I struggle at times during adversity or trials, when walking in faith and truth seems to be so hard. Give me wisdom. Give me discernment. Give me a heart that wants to know your truth. Help me to trust you and to always put your perspective above my own. Show me the value of applying truth in my daily life, and manifest in me the comfort that comes from knowing your truth, *Jehovah El Emeth*.

JEHOVAH EL GEMUWAL

LORD GOD OF RECOMPENSE

For the destroyer is coming against her, against Babylon,
And her mighty men will be captured,
Their bows are shattered;
For the LORD is a God of recompense [Jehovah El Gemuwal],
He will fully repay.

JEREMIAH 51:56

Adoration

Jehovah El Gemuwal, you are a God of recompense. You are a God who fully repays when evil is done against your own. I praise you because you are *Jehovah*, the self-existing and relational God. I praise you because you are *Elohim*, the Creator God. And I praise you because you are *Gemuwal*, the God of recompense. Because you care, you see when I am wronged. Because you create, you can restore what I have lost. Because you repay recompense, you will not leave unchecked those who have committed a foul against me. For these things and more, I lift up your name *Jehovah El Gemuwal* in blessing.

Confession

Jehovah El Gemuwal, forgive me for trying to take my own revenge. Forgive me for being afraid that you won't. Forgive me for those times when I'm angry and fearful because I'm being bullied or wronged and I forget to trust in your great name, *Jehovah El*

Gemuwal. You see all. You know all. You leave no stone unturned. I don't need to go tell everyone else when I am wronged. Rather, I need only to look to you because you will repay. You will not be mocked. Forgive me for forgetting this far too often.

Thanksgiving

Jehovah El Gemuwal, I thank you for caring. I thank you for not simply sitting on a distant throne, removed from the pain that is so real and evident in this life due to sin and sin's influence. Thank you for knowing what has happened—you know the truth—even if others cannot see it. And thank you for bringing recompense when I have been wronged, or for bringing others to repentance and then showing your mercy. Lord, you are truly holy, and your power is a beautiful thing. Thank you, again, for caring when I and those I love are wronged.

Supplication

Jehovah El Gemuwal, act. Defend the oppressed. Free those in bondage. Restore what has been lost. Repay when evil has been done. Act. Give mercy in healing, power in growth, and peace in knowing that you see, you know, and you are *Jehovah El Gemuwal.* I call on this name because you will repay and will give strength when I have been wronged. I trust this name and ask that you will manifest yourself as *Jehovah El Gemuwal* in my life.

JEHOVAH ELOHIM TSABA

LORD GOD OF HOSTS

You, O LORD God of hosts [Jehovah Elohim Tsaba],
the God of Israel,
Awake to punish all the nations;
Do not be gracious to any who are treacherous in iniquity.

PSALM 59:5

Adoration

Jehovah Elohim Tsaba, O Lord God of hosts, the God of Israel, you have power over all. You are a God of justice and might. I praise you for your skill and perfection. I bless your name for your strength and intensity. I honor you because you are *Jehovah Elohim Tsaba,* the Lord God of hosts. Armies bow before you. No weapon is stronger than you. No strategy can outwit you. No enemy can overrun you. I bless you, *Jehovah Elohim Tsaba,* as you command the armies to act on our behalf.

Confession

Jehovah Elohim Tsaba, it's easy for me to try to take matters into my own hands when I'm wronged or when I feel as if someone or something is unfair. I try to fix it or change the person or even look for ways to retaliate. Please forgive me for harboring ill feelings toward others who have mistreated me or overlooked me somehow. Instead of taking matters into my own hands, I want to remember your name, *Jehovah Elohim Tsaba,* and trust in you as the great warrior God and the Lord God of hosts. Thank you for your forgiveness, grace, and mercy in my life.

Thanksgiving

Jehovah Elohim Tsaba, thank you for being the Lord God of hosts. Thank you for making your strength available through your relationship with me. I'm grateful for each and every time you've shown up to right a wrong or defend me. I have seen your powerful hand in history, and I trust I will continue to see it in the days ahead. Thank you for your presence when I face trials and troubles in the future. Thank you for being the commander in chief of the armies and for commanding them to act on my behalf.

Supplication

Jehovah Elohim Tsaba, will you make your presence known to me in such a way that I will feel at peace? Help me not to take matters into my own hands but rather to trust you. I ask you to right any wrongs that have occurred in my life and to bring to repentance those who have wronged me. I ask you to defend me as your child and help me to rest in your care. Where I have honored you and yet still suffered, show me that you are there—that you are *Jehovah Elohim Tsaba*, the Lord God of hosts.

JEHOVAH ELOHIM YESHUA

LORD GOD OF MY SALVATION

O Lord, the God of my salvation [Jehovah Elohim Yeshua],
I have cried out by day and in the night before You.

PSALM 88:1

Adoration

Jehovah Elohim Yeshua, you are the Lord God of my salvation. You reign from heaven and rule on earth. You rescue those in need and bind up the brokenhearted. You save not only eternally but also in time and history. Through the wisdom in your Word, you save me from making wrong choices or going down the wrong path. You save me from a life of misery and regret through your healing forgiveness and grace. You save me from worry by assuring me that I can trust in you. You save me from confusion when I seek your truth and kingdom agenda in my life. I praise you because you are *Jehovah Elohim Yeshua*, the Lord God of my salvation.

Confession

Jehovah Elohim Yeshua, I confess that I sometimes try to be my own savior. Rather than look to you, I try to find my own solutions and force them into place. Rather than honor you as King, I try to place myself in a position of authority. *Jehovah Elohim Yeshua*, you are the one who saves. Forgive me for not turning to you and instead turning to my friends, family, or others to seek solutions for the trials I face. I should always turn to you first in everything.

Thanksgiving

Jehovah Elohim Yeshua, thank you for being not only a God who sits on high, and not only a God with creative powers, but also a God who humbly comes down to each one of us—even to me!—to save. By trusting in Jesus Christ for the forgiveness of my sins, I have received eternal salvation. And by trusting in you, *Jehovah Elohim Yeshua*, in my daily life, I see you saving me from unnecessary pain, confusion, waste, and regret. You are the God who saves. Thank you for inviting me to call you by the name *Jehovah Elohim Yeshua*.

Supplication

Jehovah Elohim Yeshua, I seek your salvation in my life. Save me from my own mistakes and sins. Rescue me from the consequences I've brought on myself by making wrong choices. Deliver me when others wrong me. Save me from a life of wasted hours and days, and rescue my heart from that which pains it. Show me your great hand of salvation, *Yeshua*. You delivered the Israelites from bondage in Egypt, and I believe you can lead me away from my own bondage—whether it be external or internal—and into a land of rest.

ELOHEI MIKKAROV

GOD WHO IS NEAR

"Am I a God who is near [Elohei Mikkarov],"
declares the LORD,
"And not a God far off?"

JEREMIAH 23:23

Adoration

Elohei Mikkarov, you have commanded me to be strong and courageous and to not be frightened, just as you spoke to Joshua so long ago. I am not to be dismayed because you, my *Elohei Mikkarov*, are near me wherever I go. Because of you I am able to freely live. I am able to move forward and know you are there. You are the God of my praise—the God of my presence. Where I am, you are. There is nowhere I can go outside of you. I am yours, and I honor you with the words of my mouth, lifting up my hands for all to see that you are the one who brings my heart to a place of true praise.

Confession

Elohei Mikkarov, you are near. You are not far from me, but I am sometimes far from you. When I feel distance between myself and you, you are not the one who has wandered. Forgive me for being so far away in my thoughts and in my heart. You are right here. You are with me right now. When I look for you, I find you. Yet forgive me for not seeing you when I am blinded by my own desires and my own pain. Make me know your presence, *Elohei Mikkarov*, so I can ever experience you in all that I do.

Thanksgiving

Elohei Mikkarov, thank you for being near as well as far off. I don't have to be anxious about the things I need, because you are so close you already know what I need. You stand at the door. You abide in my soul. Where can I go from your Spirit? Thank you that I cannot flee from your presence. You are the God who is close to me, and I give you my gratitude for never abandoning me and never leaving me.

Supplication

Elohei Mikkarov, may I know the grace of your presence by being aware of it. Will you cause things to happen in my life to help me recognize your nearness? I want to live my life in the full awareness of you, *Elohei Mikkarov*. I don't want to spend another day or waste another opportunity not experiencing you. The full and abundant life is found only in you. Show me your hand, your heart, your love. Give me a sign of your abiding closeness in my life.

ELOHIM CHASDI

GOD OF LOVINGKINDNESS

O my strength, I will sing praises to You;
For God is my stronghold, the God [Elohim]
who shows me lovingkindness [Chasdi].

PSALM 59:17

Adoration

Elohim Chasdi, you are compassionate and gracious, slow to anger and abounding in love. You do not harbor anger forever, nor do you treat me as my sins deserve or repay me according to my iniquities. As high as the heavens are above the earth, that is how great your love is for those who fear you. As far as the east is from the west, this is how far you have removed my transgressions from me. And as a father has compassion on his children, so you have compassion on those who fear you. I praise your name, *Elohim Chasdi*, for your lovingkindness endures forever.

Confession

Elohim Chasdi, you are my stronghold and the God who shows me lovingkindness. I confess I don't always look to you as my stronghold but rather attempt to solve my problems on my own. Forgive me for neglecting to make you the focal point when I am facing trials or heartaches. Forgive me for turning to other means for comfort instead of turning to your faithful kindness and goodness.

Thanksgiving

Elohim Chasdi, thank you for the kindness, goodness, and faithfulness you show me. Though people may disappoint me, your goodness never fails me. At times I don't understand what you're doing, but I'm thankful I can trust in your name, *Elohim Chasdi*. By faith, I thank you for working all things out for my good and my growth, even when I'm unable to understand. Thank you for your strength and for making your love available to me when I simply seek your face.

Supplication

Elohim Chasdi, give me a greater glimpse of your name today. Give me a deeper experience of your kindness, goodness, and faithfulness. Let me taste *Elohim Chasdi* in the fullest expression of who you are. Give me wisdom when I need to know you more. And then, in fully knowing you, help me express your kindness, goodness, and faithfulness to others in your name. Our world is in great need of love and kindness, *Elohim Chasdi*. Make me a vessel of your love to those in need. As you minister to others through me, fill me up with the strength of your kindness each day.

ELOHIM BASHAMAYIM

GOD IN HEAVEN

*When we heard it, our hearts melted and no courage
remained in any man any longer because of you; for
the LORD your God, He is God in heaven [Elohim
Bashamayim] above and on earth beneath.*

JOSHUA 2:11

Adoration

Elohim Bashamayim, who sits in heaven above and on earth
beneath, you are truly the ruler over all of the nations. Power and
might are in your hand, and no one can stand against you. You are
Elohim Bashamayim, who drove out the inhabitants of the land
before your people Israel and gave it to the descendants of your
friend Abraham. You have likewise gone before me to open doors
I could not open on my own, and you lead me in a path I could
not have created on my own. I stand before you and lift up your
great name, *Elohim Bashamayim*. I lift up my eyes and look to you.

Confession

Elohim Bashamayim, whatever is born of you overcomes the
world. I am born of you, and so I overcome the world. This is the
victory that overcomes the world, even my faith, because you are
Elohim Bashamayim, the God over all—the God in heaven. Forgive my little faith when it comes to living and walking in the victory you have gained for me through the cross of Jesus Christ.

Have mercy on me when I doubt your promises. You are the God of heaven. You are over all. Show me your great grace as you pardon my sins against you.

Thanksgiving

Elohim Bashamayim, I thank you for causing me to always triumph in Christ Jesus and for having given me the victory through my Savior. As the God of heaven, you own all. You know all. You are over all. Thank you for your greatness and might and yet for not forgetting about me. Rather, you desire to intimately relate to me in a loving way. Thank you, *Elohim Bashamayim*, for who you are and how you have chosen to express yourself—through the blessed gift of sending your Son, Jesus Christ, to earth so that I may know you more fully through him.

Supplication

Elohim Bashamayim, lift up your mighty arm and open your outstretched hand in my life that I may experience your power. Help me to know you more through my relationship with you, your Spirit, and your Son, Jesus Christ. I want to understand your desires so that I can make them my own desires. I want to know your will so that I can walk in the blessing and favor of your way. Grant me your favor, *Elohim Bashamayim*, because your favor is over all, and nothing can stand in the way of my destiny when your hand is upon me.

JEHOVAH HASHOPET

THE LORD, THE JUDGE

I have not wronged you, but you are doing me
wrong by waging war against me. Let the LORD, the
Judge [Jehovah Hashopet], decide the dispute this
day between the Israelites and the Ammonites.

JUDGES 11:27 NIV

Adoration

Jehovah Hashopet, sometimes people rise up against me when I have not wronged them. In the book of Judges the Israelites called to you because they had not wronged their enemy and yet their enemy was waging war against them. They appealed to you as the Judge to decide the dispute as you do so well. I praise you for your justice—your scales of fairness—and for hearing my prayer when I am in need of justice. You are a righteous God, offended by evil and wholly devoted to justice.

Confession

Jehovah Hashopet, I confess that when I am wronged, I don't always turn to you for your justice. Instead I throw myself a pity party. Forgive me for my episodes of self-pity. Help me know the confidence I can feel in your execution of judgment. Truly you are able to render justice on my behalf far better than I ever could. Please forgive me when I forget to call on you for your judgments.

Thanksgiving

Jehovah Hashopet, thank you for being a holy God, entirely righteous in all you do. Thank you for your heart of justice, which is faithful to your truth. Thank you for inviting me to turn to you when I'm in need and for assuring me that you know the truth even when falsehood is spread against me. While others seek war, my heart is for peace, and I know you see this in me. Thank you for defending me when I'm unjustly opposed.

Supplication

Jehovah Hashopet, an enemy has risen against me, an enemy I used to call and consider a friend. Only you know the person's true motivation for doing this, but I ask you to bring the truth to light and fairly judge this person for wrongly opposing me. Soften this person's heart and show them the error of their ways. Whatever they bring against me, I pray you will turn it back to them so that it might lead them to repentance. I ask for peace with this person, and I pray you will bring about this peace swiftly.

JEHOVAH HOSHIAH

O LORD, SAVE

LORD, give victory [Jehovah Hoshiah] to the king!
Answer us when we call!

PSALM 20:9 NIV

Adoration

Jehovah Hoshiah, you are the God who saves me from the pit
and who crowns me with lovingkindness and the great depth of
your compassion. You have rescued me from the domain of darkness and transferred me to your kingdom of light. I bless your
name, for you save me when I call. In your hands rests the power
of the universe. You hold all things together, and in you all things
are given life. Because of this, you alone have the power to save,
and I look to you for your divine intervention, offering you the
praise of my lips.

Confession

Jehovah Hoshiah, I come to you on behalf of our nation and
confess the communal sins we have committed. We have not
looked to your hand for salvation in such a long time, and now we
face desperate situations in the economy, in public safety, in education, and more. Look on this land and forgive us for not calling
on your name in times of need. Have mercy on us as a nation and
restore our hearts and our minds to you.

Thanksgiving

Jehovah Hoshiah, thank you for saving me when I call on you. Thank you for this aspect of your character, which is faithful and true. With gratitude I offer you this prayer of thanksgiving for all you have done and are doing in my life. Most importantly, thank you for saving me from my sins by sending your Son, Jesus Christ.

Supplication

Jehovah Hoshiah, I look to you today to save me from the mess I'm in. Some of the mess is my fault, and some of it isn't. But I ask you to intervene and give me the grace to trust you with the results. Keep my hands from trying to save myself. Instead, help me to look to you to save me. Reverse this present misfortune in my life and bring about blessing instead. Give me eyes to see where you are leading me and a compassionate heart toward others who are experiencing messes in their lives. Use me to encourage someone today as you so faithfully have encouraged me. And show me the way everlasting so that I can walk according to your will. O Lord, look with mercy and save. Bind up this broken heart and heal. Mend my wounds and cover them with your ointment of loving grace.

JEHOVAH IMMEKA

THE LORD IS WITH YOU

When the angel of the LORD appeared to Gideon, he said,
"The LORD is with you [Jehovah Immeka], mighty warrior."

JUDGES 6:12 NIV

Adoration

Jehovah Immeka, your presence alone is enough to defeat an army. When the angel of the Lord appeared to Gideon and told him you were with him, that wasn't just a soothing statement to make him feel better. That was a powerful truth that would take Gideon to a new level of courage and lead him to a military conquest of unprecedented valor. Your presence gives confidence. It also gives insight into how and what the opposition is thinking. Your presence is worth more than the presence of 30,000 strong warriors, as you demonstrated in Gideon's battle.

Confession

Jehovah Immeka, I am not alone, for you are with me. At times I feel alone, but your Word tells me that you will never leave me or abandon me. There are days when I act as if I am alone and I tend to worry or fret over things in my life. On these days especially, I seek your forgiveness for doubting your presence and your Word. Forgive me for hiding, just as Gideon did in the winepress, fearful of what life has coming at me rather than boldly approaching your throne of grace and asking for you to lead me each step of the way.

Thanksgiving

Jehovah Immeka, thank you for being with me in the morning when I wake up, in my sleep when I am dreaming, and throughout my day. Thank you for never leaving me alone and for your promise never to forsake me. I may feel alone at times, but such feelings are not based on truth. Even in the silence, you are with me. Even when I cannot hear or see your presence, you are there, just as your Word promises me. Thank you for your presence, which empowers me to defeat any enemy, overcome any obstacle, and secure any victory in my emotions, my finances, my body, my relationships, my family, and any other area of life. Thank you for the kindness of your close presence.

Supplication

Jehovah Immeka, when you are with me as you were with Gideon, you make a way where I had no way to accomplish your will. Gideon didn't have any training as a warrior, and yet you asked him to lead an army—a small army, but still an army. I ask for the confidence of Gideon—for the assurance of your response when I put out a fleece and then put it out again. Take me to greater heights in my life and more valiant victories by reminding me of your strong presence and the power that comes from abiding with you. You promise that if I ask anything according to your will, you will give it, so I ask boldly today for you to accomplish everything you desire to do in and through my life.

SAR SHALOM

PRINCE OF PEACE

For a child will be born to us, a son will be given to us;
And the government will rest on His shoulders;
And His name will be called
Wonderful Counselor, Mighty God,
Eternal Father, Prince of Peace [Sar Shalom].

ISAIAH 9:6

Adoration

Sar Shalom, you are the prince of peace. You hold this world together simply by your intent. Where there is chaos, you bring calm. Where there are struggles, you bring stability. You alone embody peace and can bring peace to our lives, our homes, our churches, our communities, and our nation. The mere mention of your name ushers in a certain stillness. You alone know what is needed to bring about order and tranquility. You are worthy of my highest praise and adulation.

Confession

Sar Shalom, just as the disciples couldn't rest on the boat when a storm arose, sometimes I worry and fret during my personal storms. Yet in the midst of the stormy sea, you slept. You slept in peace because you are peace, and storms carry no authority over you. Forgive me for living a sleepless life on so many stormy occasions and for failing to rest in your peace. I confess that peace is sometimes elusive, and I beg your forgiveness for not letting go and letting you reign peacefully in my life.

Thanksgiving

Sar Shalom, I lift up my tired and worn-out heart to you in gratitude for your gift of peace. You calm the storms with but a word and subdue enemies with but a stone, and you offer me peace throughout my days. Thank you for this greatest of blessings. Thank you for the rest that comes by abiding in your presence, *Sar Shalom*. I don't need to fight or fret, but rather to rest in your peace. Even when I don't understand the circumstances around me and life seems unfair, you have a way of bringing a peace that calms all my confusions. It is a beautiful thing, and I thank you for it.

Supplication

Sar Shalom, give me peace when I'm prone to worry. Give me peace when I'm tempted to doubt. Fill my mind with your thoughts of peace to such a degree that my face, my muscles, my nonverbal expressions—my body language—reflect this peace to those around me. That alone would be a great victory, and I trust you to do this in my life. I ask for peace in my relationships—where there is conflict, bring resolution and restoration. I ask for peace in my heart—where there is doubt, bitterness, or regret, I ask for wisdom and acceptance within. Let my words bring peace to those around me. And bring about peace between the races and ethnicities in the world and in my nation. Quell the violence with your peace as only you can.

JEHOVAH JIREH

THE LORD WILL PROVIDE

So Abraham called that place The Lord Will Provide
[Jehovah Jireh]. And to this day it is said, "On the
mountain of the Lord it will be provided."

GENESIS 22:14 NIV

Adoration

Jehovah Jireh, my provider, your grace is adequate for all my needs. Those who seek your face on the mountain of the Lord find you there and find you sufficient in all things. You truly supply all of my needs from your abundant riches in glory. You have not left me wanting. Even at times when I've experienced lack, you have come through not only to meet my needs but also to bless me with something special—to let me know you see and you care. You are the great providing God. You give air for the lungs to breathe, light for the eyes to see, rain for the crops to grow, and love for the heart to live. You are an awesome God, worthy of all praise.

Confession

Jehovah Jireh, how many times have I looked to something else as my source when you alone are my provider? Everyone and everything else is merely a resource, yet in my humanness, I still go elsewhere for what only you can provide. How wrong of me to feel fearful at work if someone isn't happy with me or to feel fearful at home if I don't see how my bills are going to be paid. Forgive me for my audacity in thinking that the government has more control than you or that the doctor has the final say regarding my health. You are my source. You are my *Jehovah Jireh*, my provider and my Lord.

Thanksgiving

Jehovah Jireh, thank you for your provision. Thank you for not skipping a beat. In fact, if you forgot to have my heart beat as it does for even a very short while, I would no longer experience the goodness of life in the land of the living. Thank you for taking care of everything through your provision—my finances, health, food, shelter, love...all of it ultimately comes from you. Every good and perfect gift comes from above, from *Jehovah Jireh*, who provides for us all. Thank you for each and every thing—even for the difficult trials that strengthen my spiritual muscles and draw me closer to you.

Supplication

Jehovah Jireh, my provider, I think I appeal to this name more than any other. I frequently ask you to give me this or that, and I come once again doing the same. Yet I ask you to give to me only what will produce the greatest growth in me and the most far-reaching impact for your kingdom on earth. You revealed yourself as *Jehovah Jireh* when you met Abraham on the mountain just as he was about to sacrifice the pride of his life, his son Isaac, to you. Too often I forget the gravity of the situation when you first shared this name. Instead, I look to you as a cosmic genie, ready to dispense favors at my command. Let me know you in the truest and most authentic form of this name, *Jehovah Jireh*, as you meet me in my pain, sacrifice, and dedication to you. Let me see you on the mountaintop of my own struggles. Come through for me as you did in providing Abraham's sacrifice.

JEHOVAH KANNA SHEMO

THE LORD WHOSE NAME IS JEALOUS

*Do not worship any other god, for the LORD, whose name
is Jealous [Jehovah Kanna Shemo], is a jealous God.*

EXODUS 34:14 NIV

Adoration

Jehovah Kanna Shemo, your name is Jealous. You have a reason
for not wanting me to worship any other god or idol—it's because
you are the only one, true, living God. You carry the weight of the
world on your shoulders, you tell the stars where to hang, and you
deliver your children from harm. You are a present help in trouble
and a peaceful comfort when I'm alone. You deserve to be a jealous
God because you own everything, and everything comes from you.

Confession

Jehovah Kanna Shemo, I admit I don't normally associate this
name with you. If I did, I would be far more careful to show you
the honor and the respect due you. To my shame, I find I give my
time and energy to entertaining or distracting myself most of the
week, and I give you only a portion of my time. Forgive me for
such an imbalance in the order of my days. It definitely doesn't
reflect your call to kingdom living, which is to seek you first above
and before all. Thank you for your forgiveness and your mercy.

Thanksgiving

Jehovah Kanna Shemo, thank you for the grace you show me each moment of every day. As a jealous God, you have withheld much of your frustration and anger with me when I've been dismissive of you. You don't rant or rave. Instead you seek my attention in the most effective ways. Thank you for loving me so much that you are jealous of my affections.

Supplication

Jehovah Kanna Shemo, I really do want to put you first in my life and my heart—in my thoughts, actions, and desires. It seems like an easy thing to do, but I continue to put myself first. I pray that you will be kind in how you draw me closer to you and how you turn my heart toward yours. Help me to not make you jealous. Give me a heart like David's—like yours.

JEHOVAH MACHSI

THE LORD MY REFUGE

If you say, "The LORD is my refuge [Jehovah Machsi],"
and you make the Most High your dwelling,
no harm will overtake you,
no disaster will come near your tent.

PSALM 91:9-10 NIV

Adoration

Jehovah Machsi, as I dwell in your shelter, I will abide in your shadow. You truly are my refuge and my fortress, my God in whom I trust. You are the one who delivers me from the snare of the trapper and from the deadly pestilence. You cover me with your pinions, and under your wings I seek my refuge—your faithfulness is a shield and bulwark. Because of you, I am not afraid of the terror by night or of the arrow that flies by day, of the pestilence that stalks in the darkness or of the destruction that lays waste at noon. I have made you, *Jehovah Machsi*, my refuge, even my dwelling place.

Confession

There is power in the name *Jehovah Machsi* to free me from that which holds me in bondage. Forgive me for not accessing that power on a regular basis—for worrying, fearing, having anxiety, trying to figure it all out on my own, and much more. Rather than simply resting in your refuge, I try to fix it, change it, move it, overcome it…all in my own strength, which leaves me only frustrated at the end of the day. May I know you as my refuge and abide in your truth and power.

Thanksgiving

Jehovah Machsi, thank you for being my refuge. You are my dwelling place, my home. Thank you for showing me where I can go when I feel lost, lonely, or abandoned. Thank you for shielding me from the storms of life and guiding me through the trials I face. Thank you, *Jehovah Machsi*, for breaking every chain in my life, freeing me from the bondage of legalism, anxiety, disappointment, perfectionism, fear, and much more. I can feel the chains fall as I run into your refuge, and I give you my gratitude for your presence and help.

Supplication

Jehovah Machsi, show me where you are. Show me where my refuge is. I often run to distractions—things to take my mind off of what I'm dealing with—but I want you to stand in front of me just as clearly as the angel stood in front of Baalam and the donkey. Open my eyes so I can see you just as clearly as Elisha's servant saw your army. Show me my refuge that I may run there each and every time I need to. There is power in your name, *Jehovah Machsi*, and I want to experience it.

JEHOVAH MAGEN

THE LORD MY SHIELD

Blessed are you, O Israel;
Who is like you, a people saved by the LORD [Jehovah],
Who is the shield [Magen] of your help
And the sword of your majesty!
So your enemies will cringe before you,
And you will tread upon their high places.

DEUTERONOMY 33:29

Adoration

Jehovah Magen, blessed is your name. Blessed is your ability to shield your people and to save. You bring help when help is needed. You bring protection when protection is requested. You enable your own to tread on the heights just as you lifted the Israelites above their enemies when their hearts were turned toward you. No army is too big to intimidate you. No evil plan can outwit you. Enemies cower before you because you are *Jehovah Magen*.

Confession

Jehovah Magen, forgive me for running out from behind your shield, for not putting you first in my life. You say that if I will seek first your kingdom and your righteousness, all the things I need will be given to me, including your shield of protection. Yet I've put a number of things ahead of you and ultimately stepped away so many times. *Jehovah Magen*, you are like an umbrella, shielding me from the rain. You don't make the rain stop all the time. Sometimes you allow it to continue. But when I am under you as my umbrella, you stop the rain from falling on me. Forgive me for stepping out from under your covering and seeking my own.

Thanksgiving

Jehovah Magen, thank you for the goodness of your protecting power and for the greatness of your strength. A shield is able to defend only if it is large enough, strong enough, and positioned correctly. You are all of these things, and I'm grateful that you offer yourself to me as my *Magen*, the shield of my life.

Supplication

Jehovah Magen, shield me from the attacks of the enemy. He comes at me with fiery darts, seeking to remove me from your will, harden my heart to your love, and lure me into temptation and sin. Restore to me a spirit of faith so that I will look to your shield in every way. Shield me from attacks that come when I am believing a lie and not the truth. I am a child of the King and an heir to your kingdom, and I ask you to be my shield from anything and everything that tries to get me to believe differently.

JEHOVAH MAUZZI

THE LORD MY FORTRESS

LORD [Jehovah], my strength and my fortress [Mauzzi],
my refuge in time of distress,
to you the nations will come
from the ends of the earth and say,
"Our ancestors possessed nothing but false gods,
worthless idols that did them no good."

JEREMIAH 16:19 NIV

Adoration

Jehovah Mauzzi, you are my strength and my fortress, my refuge in time of distress. To you the nations will come from the ends of the earth and declare that their ancestors possessed nothing but false gods, worthless idols that did them no good. On that day, all people will come to you and bow their knees. They will acknowledge you as the one true God—the fortress who stands higher and longer than all man-made fortresses because you are the great eternal God.

Confession

Jehovah Mauzzi, I bless your name, for you are my wall of defense, my ready-made protection and my fortress. In you I find relief from my trials and tribulations. Forgive me for not praising you as I should for protecting me from so many dangers over the years. You have prevented events and situations that would have harmed me. You kept them from reaching me, yet I have not adored or worshipped you in gratitude for being my fortress, as I should have.

Thanksgiving

Jehovah Mauzzi, my fortress and my God, thank you for already knowing what to do. You already know what's going to happen to me, and you are directing my steps in your great kingdom plan. Thank you for your strength, wisdom, power, and protection. Because of you, I do not fear the many things I would fear apart from faith in you. Because of you, I am able to enjoy my life, assured of your presence and refuge. You are my strength when I am weary, and I thank you for infusing me with your strong presence.

Supplication

Jehovah Mauzzi, let your name be praised in all the lands. Give new missionaries a desire to go into the world to tell of your great protection. Bring the nations to you that they may know you and see that the gods and idols they've trusted in have led them only into destruction. Give me wisdom to know the best way to contribute in my community and in my country to glorify your name, *Jehovah Mauzzi*, and to spread the word of your protection. Give me boldness and opportunities to make a difference on earth for your kingdom so that many people can experience you as their fortress.

JEHOVAH HA-MELECH

THE LORD, THE KING

With trumpets and the blast of the ram's horn—
shout for joy before the LORD, the King [Jehovah Ha-Melech].

PSALM 98:6 NIV

Adoration

Jehovah Ha-Melech, I stand before you with my arms wide open
and my heart humbled. I shout for joy before you, for you are my
King. I bow my head and give you the reverence you deserve. I proclaim to all that I am yours. Yes, I belong to you, O *Jehovah Ha-
Melech.* I have placed everything I am into your kingly hands, and
I give all of me to all of you. With honor, I lift up your name. With
praise, I applaud you for all you are and all you have done.

Confession

Jehovah Ha-Melech, I confess how often I place myself as my
own ruler instead of looking to you as my King. I make my own
decisions. I follow my own words. I choose my own wisdom. As
a result, I reap my own consequences. O *Jehovah Ha-Melech,* forgive my audacity for trying to usurp your rightful place in my life.
Please pardon my iniquity and take your rightful place as King of
my heart.

Thanksgiving

Jehovah Ha-Melech, thank you for the hope you give to me in knowing you as ruler over all. The peace I experience in my life is a result of your hand. The blessings you give, you give because you are over all. You are not a King to be slighted nor ignored. You are a King who is rightfully due the greatest praise, honor, and thanksgiving possible. Thank you, *Jehovah Ha-Melech*, for who you are and for humbling yourself to meet me time and time again in the midst of my struggles, doubts, and pain. Thank you for lifting me up once again, *Jehovah Ha-Melech*.

Supplication

Jehovah Ha-Melech, I seek your presence, for in your presence is freedom. In your presence is peace. You are all I need, my King. May your kingdom come. May your will be done. May all that you desire be brought to bear on earth as it is in heaven. As a nation, as a community, as a church, as a family, and I myself—may we align ourselves underneath you to show you how much we honor and respect who you are and how we long for you to reign in all we do.

PELEH YO'ETZ

WONDERFUL COUNSELOR

For to us a child is born,
to us a son is given,
and the government will be on his shoulders.
And he will be called
Wonderful Counselor [Peleh Yo'etz], Mighty God,
Everlasting Father, Prince of Peace.

Isaiah 9:6 niv

Adoration

Peleh Yo'etz, your wisdom gives life. When I lack wisdom, you tell me to simply ask you, and you will give it freely and abundantly. This is because you are my Wonderful Counselor. You are the one to guide me in the path that will bring fruit, peace, and life. Your counsel is pure, then peaceable, gentle, open to reason, full of mercy and good fruits, impartial and sincere. Breathe over me, *Peleh Yo'etz*, and let your counsel take root deep within my soul. Let your thoughts guide and direct my steps in all I do. Keep me from my own futility of mind, my own shortsightedness. Let me honor and respect your timing, your purpose, and your counsel in my life.

Confession

Peleh Yo'etz, I have access to the greatest counsel and the deepest wisdom available to man. And yet on most days, I make my own decisions based on my own finite thoughts. Forgive me for not seeking you in all I do. Forgive me for not knowing this name of yours on a moment-by-moment basis and opening up the floodgates of your counsel and wisdom into my soul by digging into your Word and seeking your face.

Thanksgiving

Peleh Yo'etz, thank you for blessing me with your counsel and understanding. Wisdom from you is better than silver or gold. What you have to give to me is more precious than jewels. Long life is in your right hand, and in your left hand is the honor I seek. Thank you for making your ways pleasant and your paths peaceful.

Supplication

Peleh Yo'etz, I see the open door that gives me access to come to you, and I seek counsel in all I do. I ask you to take my hand and draw me to you. Speak in a way I can easily discern, Lord. Teach me how to hear your counsel. Demonstrate how important it is for me to follow it. Grant me success in all I do as I commit my way, my path, and my decisions to you. Let me not boast in anything except knowing you and understanding you, for you are the one who practices steadfast love, justice, and righteousness in the earth. You are the one who counsels what is right, and you delight in offering your wisdom to all.

JEHOVAH MEPHALTI

THE LORD MY DELIVERER

The LORD [Jehovah] is my rock, my fortress
and my deliverer [Mephalti];
my God is my rock, in whom I take refuge,
my shield and the horn of my salvation, my stronghold.

PSALM 18:2 NIV

Adoration

Jehovah Mephalti, you are the deliverer. You are the fortress. You are the rock. Whoever is in you is saved. The thief comes only to steal and kill and destroy. But you came that I may have life and have it to its fullest. I praise you, for you are holy. I praise you, for you are powerful. I praise you, for you are my deliverer. You are my Lord. I can hear you calling. I can feel your glory. I can see you rise up and be my strength. Receive my praise; receive all that is within me, for I give you the highest honor of my heart.

Confession

Jehovah Mephalti, sometimes fear and anxiety creep into my thoughts. Whether they are gripping or subtle, they come to cause me to doubt your power, might, and delivering hand. I turn my thoughts to what might be, what could happen, or what I could lose rather than trusting in your sovereign hand and power. Too much time has been lost in worry or fear. Too many moments that could have been redeemed have gone into waste, just as the enemy wanted. Forgive me, *Jehovah Mephalti*, for ignoring your deliverance in times of distress.

Thanksgiving

Jehovah Mephalti, nothing can come to me that doesn't first pass through your hands. Nothing can pierce me that hasn't received your permission. Those are easy words to say, but in the moment, when I'm facing fear and doubt, they're not so easy to live out. Thank you for the kindness you show me in those times to remind me that you are my deliverer. Thank you for not giving up on me. Thank you for coming to me and whispering time and again your promises of deliverance.

Supplication

Jehovah Mephalti, life is fragile. Every day on the news we hear of a new tragedy or of a life cut short due to humanity's sin. Attacks come, whether they are emotional, financial, physical—any number of things—and life can take its toll. These things can rob me of my joy, hope, and peace. *Jehovah Mephalti*, may I ever remember this name. May this name be at the forefront of my mind so I will know with the fullest assurance that you are here as my deliverer, that you are stronger and more powerful than anything that comes against me. Give me the peace that comes with trust. Give me the grace that comes with hope.

JEHOVAH MEKADDISHKEM

THE LORD WHO SANCTIFIES YOU

*Speak to the sons of Israel, saying, "You shall surely observe
My sabbaths; for this is a sign between Me and you
throughout your generations, that you may know that I am
the LORD who sanctifies you [Jehovah Mekaddishkem]."*

EXODUS 31:13

Adoration

Jehovah Mekaddishkem, you are the God who sanctifies me. I
pray you will sanctify me in your truth, for your Word is truth.
You are the God of peace, who sanctifies me completely. May my
whole spirit, soul, and body be kept blameless at your coming,
Lord Jesus Christ. I praise you, for you have kept me as your own,
set apart to your work—sanctified to do your will. Receive the
honor I give to you, and may the fruit of my lips bring you joy.

Confession

Jehovah Mekaddishkem, remember me with grace and mercy.
I ask you to show me kindness and great forgiveness for giving
myself to things that are not holy. Forgive me for taking what you
have set apart as your own and using it on profane things. Forgive
my lack of honor toward my own life in many ways—a life you
have bought and paid for at a great cost. Show me the greatest of
mercy for not treating as sanctified that which you have sanctified.

Thanksgiving

Jehovah Mekaddishkem, thank you for making me yours. Thank you for setting me apart to be your own. You are holy. You are beautiful. You are kind. I place all I am into your loving hands and ask you to keep me in the shelter of your wings. Sanctify me in the hope that comes from knowing you are the one who is sovereign over all. I give you my thoughts, my talents, and my time. Sanctify all according to the purpose you have ordained for me. Use my skills and talents to glorify you. Allow my words to be set apart for you. Thank you for showing me I have a destiny to serve your kingdom purposes and advance your glory on earth.

Supplication

Jehovah Mekaddishkem, you have sanctified me, and I am yours. You have chosen me as your ambassador on earth. I shout out your name, my Lord. I proclaim to all that I am yours. All that I am is yours. May you be pleased to use me for your good and for your glory. Open the doors I need to go through. Close the doors that I should not step through. Set me apart to accomplish everything you have chosen for me to do. And may I forever be kept close to you in all I do. Forgive me when I fail and quickly return me to the path you have chosen for me.

JEHOVAH METSUDHATHI

THE LORD MY HIGH TOWER

The LORD [Jehovah] is my rock,
my fortress [Metsudhathi] and my deliverer;
my God is my rock, in whom I take refuge,
my shield and the horn of my salvation, my stronghold.

PSALM 18:2 NIV

Adoration

Jehovah Metsudhathi, you are my rock, my fortress, and my deliverer. You are the one in whom I take refuge. When I'm up against a wall and the enemy is aiming his fiery darts at me to try to take me down, you, *Jehovah Metsudhathi*, are my shield. I lift up your name in praise because you alone are the horn of my salvation and my stronghold. Nothing else can deliver me from the evil clutch of death that threatens my hopes, dreams, and relationships. In you alone I find my high tower, to which I run for safety

Confession

Jehovah Metsudhathi, I often feel squeezed by life's demands and pressures, and I forget to put my trust in you. God, I'm sorry for being so shortsighted and letting my trials and fears overwhelm my thoughts to such a degree that I neglect to run to you, my high tower, with every need I have. Have mercy on me and know that I put my hope in you in all things—it's just that I forget sometimes when my emotions run high. Remind me in those times of your ever-present help in times of trouble.

Thanksgiving

Jehovah Metsudhathi, thank you for your strength. Thank you for your might. Thank you for providing a place for me to run to in my times of need. Thank you, my God, for not abandoning me to my own devices. You provide a way out of my troubles even where there seems to be no way. Thank you for reminding me at those times when I forget to call on you, O King. Teach me to hear your voice and to respond to you during my hardest days.

Supplication

Jehovah Metsudhathi, I want to take this time in prayer today to pray for those who don't know you as their high tower, the one who is waiting to provide them with help and hope. Lord, I lift up to you my family members and friends who are not close to you. I ask you to draw them to you with your loving care. Show them that in the midst of their trials and tribulations, you are there for them, ever ready to provide a shield against life's storms. Open my mouth when I am with them to share of your steadfast love and care, and make me a witness of your hope to those in need.

JEHOVAH MOSHIEKH

THE LORD YOUR SAVIOR

I will make your oppressors eat their own flesh;
they will be drunk on their own blood, as with wine.
Then all mankind will know
that I, the LORD [Jehovah], am your Savior [Moshiekh],
your Redeemer, the Mighty One of Jacob.

ISAIAH 49:26 NIV

Adoration

Jehovah Moshiekh, you are indeed my Savior. You have already conquered my greatest foe—Satan. You have done as you said you would and have saved me from his hands of oppression. You are the King of this kingdom, the Ruler over all. The enemy thought he could overcome you when he sought to destroy all of the newborns at the time Christ was born. He was unsuccessful. Then he sought to destroy Jesus on the cross at Calvary. But he was unsuccessful there too. I give you praise, for you are the ultimate victor over all, and you can save me from that which seeks to destroy me as well.

Confession

Jehovah Moshiekh, forgive me for failing to share the good news of your salvation with as many people as I can. Forgive me for not speaking up in times when I should share the importance of what you have done. You are the Savior of the world—the mighty God, who not only creates but also saves. Give me the grace to sense when you are opening doors in the life of someone who needs to know you—someone I know—so that I might speak up and tell them of your goodness and mercy. Help me to pray more fervently for the lost so they may come to know you as their Savior.

Thanksgiving

Jehovah Moshiekh, this is perhaps that name I most take for granted. Thank you for being my Savior. Thank you for coming to my defense—for loving me before I loved you in return. Thank you for paying the price for my sins when Jesus Christ suffered on the cross to afford me not only eternal salvation but also sanctification in my everyday life. My greatest thanksgiving surrounds this name as I lift it up to you in humble praise. Receive my gratitude and know that I'm truly thankful for your salvation in my daily life and for all of eternity.

Supplication

Jehovah Moshiekh, make me a vessel of your salvation to those who need to know you. Make my life a living testimony that speaks of your grace and mercy. Show me how to live. Teach me what to say so I will glorify you in all I do. I pray that when others see your salvation in my life, they will be encouraged to receive it in theirs as well. Let me not waste my days or hours—teach me how to pray for those who need you, and to follow through by speaking to them of your great saving power.

JEHOVAH NISSI

THE LORD MY BANNER

Moses built an altar and named it
The LORD is My Banner [Jehovah Nissi].

EXODUS 17:15

Adoration

Jehovah Nissi, I worship you out of a heart of gratitude for being the banner over my life. When I face trials and troubles, I know I can look to you to cover me. Your covenantal covering protects me and guides me in a world that's sometimes dangerous and filled with troubles. You have said that in this world I will face tribulation but that you have overcome the world. Because of your power to overcome, you are my banner when I need you the most. Receive my praise and adoration as I lift up your name in love.

Confession

Jehovah Nissi, I have wasted many minutes, hours, and days fearing for things that I should have looked to you to handle. Worry does nothing for me—it only prolongs the stress. Yet you have stood by, waiting to guide and protect me as my banner and my covering. Lord, forgive me for all the times I have doubted in my heart and mind by turning to my fears rather than turning to you. You promise that I will find you if I will seek you. I seek you today, *Jehovah Nissi*, as my banner and my victory.

Thanksgiving

Jehovah Nissi, thank you for the goodness you provide and the security you offer those who trust in you. You are strong and mighty and able to defeat any enemy. Thank you for standing with me in my thoughts as I struggle with decisions I've made in the past—decisions that have filled me with regret. Thank you for being my banner and for helping me to move forward and let the past be the past. If I will delight myself in you, you will give me the desires of my heart and put me on the path to the destiny you have created me to fulfill.

Supplication

Jehovah Nissi, you are my banner. Without you the storms of life come upon me and often overwhelm me. We live in such a fragile world—our emotions, our health, and our relationships are fragile at times. I know you are good and you are strong, so I ask you to help that knowledge translate into my emotions. Then I will feel secure and at peace in the midst of life's storms as I look to you, my banner—my *Jehovah Nissi*—as my strong and righteous arm.

JEHOVAH ORI

THE LORD MY LIGHT

The LORD [Jehovah] is my light [Ori] and my salvation—
whom shall I fear?
The Lord is the stronghold of my life—
of whom shall I be afraid?

PSALM 27:1 NIV

Adoration

Jehovah Ori, you are the light of my life. You are the shining star brightening my path. I praise you for helping each of us to navigate through the darkness of this life. You are the pure light. You are holy. You are strong. I lift up your name in adoration and praise, giving you the worth you are due. I sing to you in honor and gratitude for your greatness. May your name be exalted among the nations. May your praise be lifted up throughout the land. Draw people to you so that they may know and experience you as the light of their lives.

Confession

Jehovah Ori, how many hours have I spent trying to figure out my own way? How many times have I tried to Google my solutions or call a friend rather than turn to you in humble surrender and acknowledge that you alone are the light, that you alone know the way? Forgive me for wasted emotions, energy, and time. Forgive me for being so consumed with my own darkness that I forget you are there as my light and my salvation. You are *Jehovah Ori*, and you know the path I should take. Show me your grace and your goodness. Light my way.

Thanksgiving

Jehovah Ori, you are worthy of all of my thanksgiving. Thank you for your patience as you show me the path I should take and lead me to your Word, which reveals your will in my life. When I'm consumed by my own troubles, you find a way to communicate with me and remind me of who you are. You remind me that you are *Jehovah Ori* and that you want to light my way. You bring me the light of salvation if only I turn to you with a heart of trust. Receive my gratitude for your greatness.

Supplication

Jehovah Ori, sometimes the decisions I need to make overwhelm me. I want to make the right decision, but I can't foresee all of the consequences of my choices—both good and bad. I don't have enough wisdom to know which job I should take, which house I should buy, which relationship I should nurture…Whatever the decision is, *Jehovah Ori*, will you shine a light on the path I'm to take and show me which way I should go?

JEHOVAH UZZI

THE LORD MY STRENGTH

The LORD [Jehovah] is my strength [Uzzi] and my shield;
My heart trusts in Him, and I am helped;
Therefore my heart exults,
And with my song I shall thank Him.

PSALM 28:7

Adoration

Jehovah Uzzi, with you I can do all things because you are my strength. I praise you for the power you provide to those who place their trust in you. Because of you, I'm able to do that which I cannot on my own. You ask me to be strong and courageous, and you even become my strength as I engage in battles. You will never leave me, nor will you forsake me. I lift up your name in praise and adoration for being my strength.

Confession

Jehovah Uzzi, my own strength cannot compare with your strength, and yet I often rely on myself when hard times come. I frequently look to my own might and power or applaud my own abilities when victories are won. How quickly I forget that it is not by might nor by power but by your Spirit in me that I overcome the obstacles in my life. Forgive me for not relying on your strength. Forgive me also when I seek to take the credit for my victory when the credit is truly due to you.

Thanksgiving

Jehovah Uzzi, I never need to fear because you are with me. Neither do I need to be dismayed because you are my God—you strengthen me and help me, upholding me with your righteous right hand. In you I find all I need to fully live out my destiny. Thank you for being my strength. But even greater than that, thank you for the peace I have knowing I can rest in this truth.

Supplication

Jehovah Uzzi, help me wait for you because your Word tells me that those who wait on you will renew their strength. They will mount up with wings like eagles—running without growing weary and walking without getting faint. Show me the reward of patience—the power of truly waiting to see your strength manifested in my life. Grant me the virtue of relying on you in all I do, for when I am weak, you are strong. I want to walk and run in that truth.

JEHOVAH ROPHE

THE LORD OUR HEALER

*He said, "If you listen carefully to the LORD your God
and do what is right in his eyes, if you pay attention to
his commands and keep all his decrees, I will not bring
on you any of the diseases I brought on the Egyptians, for
I am the LORD, who heals [Jehovah Rophe] you."*

EXODUS 15:26 NIV

Adoration

Jehovah Rophe, in your Word you told the Israelites that if they
worshipped you as their Lord and God, you would bless their
bread and water and take sickness away from them. I lift your
name in praise and adoration because you are the ultimate care-
giver. With just one word, you can remove sickness, reverse disease,
and bring healing in the cells of our bodies. You hold the ultimate
power in your hands. We may look to physicians or to medicine
to heal us, but you have the final say. I praise you for your power
and for your willingness and ability to heal.

Confession

Jehovah Rophe, forgive me for not trusting in your healing
power and for worrying and fretting about what might be wrong
in my body or in a relative's body. Heal me not only of physical ail-
ments, I pray, but also of the doubt that keeps me from trusting in
you as *Jehovah Rophe* and looking to you as my healer. Forgive me

for harming my body by not eating well, exercising consistently, or resting enough. Forgive me for not treasuring my body and treating it with the value that it deserves as your creation and temple.

Thanksgiving

Jehovah Rophe, you tell me to be attentive to your words and to incline my ear to your sayings. To not let them escape from my sight but to keep them within my heart. You tell me this because they are life to me and healing to my flesh. When I cry to you in the time of trouble, you save me from my distress by sending out your word and healing me. Thank you for your steadfast love and for your wonderful work in my life.

Supplication

Jehovah Rophe, heal me. Heal my heart where bitterness has taken hold. Heal my body where sickness has crept in. Heal my soul where doubt plagues me. Heal my hope when I have given up. *Jehovah Rophe*, heal me. Heal my words so I will speak kindness to those I meet. Heal my thoughts so I will think on that which is lovely. Show me how to care for the body you have given to me— what to eat, when to eat, what to drink, how much to rest, and how much to exercise. Make me aware of the importance of taking care of that which you have freely given to me to enjoy—my life.

JEHOVAH ROHI

THE LORD MY SHEPHERD

The LORD is my shepherd [Jehovah Rohi], I lack nothing.
PSALM 23:1 NIV

Adoration

Jehovah Rohi, you are my shepherd, so I shall not be in want. You make me to lie down in green pastures. You restore my soul. You lead me beside still waters. You prepare a table for me in the presence of those who oppose me. You anoint my head with oil and cause my cup to overflow. Because of you, goodness and mercy will follow me all of the days of my life. Because you are my shepherd, I will dwell in your house forever. You are the great shepherd. You are the guider of my soul. You are both King and shepherd over all.

Confession

Jehovah Rohi, I often feel as if I am in want. I often look at things I don't have and covet them. Forgive me for my discontent. As my shepherd, you've given me all I need. When I feel lack, it's not because you haven't provided for me. It's because I've disregarded what you have given. Pardon my sins, especially when they rise up in the face of all the blessings you've given me. I must seem like an ungrateful child to you at times, and for that I ask for your forgiveness and grace.

Thanksgiving

Jehovah Rohi, thank you for being so patient and kind. Thank you for leading me to green pastures and making me lie down there. You know where I will thrive, and you guide me there. You find the place of deepest rest and open up the door for me. Thank you for constantly looking out for my well-being even when I'm not doing so myself. Thank you for thinking for me when I fail to think for myself. I've seen your hand of intervention throughout my life—closing doors that would have been harmful to me if I had gone through them. Thank you for being my shepherd, who knows what's best and leads me in that direction.

Supplication

Jehovah Rohi, with all the confusion ahead of me, I need you to guide me on the right path. I can't always see which way to go and what decision to make. I need you to be my shepherd and show me the way. Will you help me learn how to listen to you even better than I do now? Will you tune my heart and mind to hear your voice so I will more easily follow you, just as a trusting lamb follows its shepherd? Help me make decisions that honor you and bring you glory. Without you as my shepherd, I would surely wander and eventually get lost. Guide me with your hand and show me your loving care as you shepherd me through life's path.

RUACH HAKKODESH

HOLY SPIRIT

*Do not cast me away from Your presence
And do not take Your Holy Spirit
[Ruach Hakkodesh] from me.*

PSALM 51:11

Adoration

Ruach Hakkodesh, you are the essence and being of God. You represent him and reflect him in so many ways. I lift you up in praise and I worship your beautiful holiness. I kneel before you, *Ruach Hakkodesh*, and lift up my hands to you, proclaiming to all who will hear that I belong to you and that I honor you with my thoughts, words, and actions. All that I am, I give to you. All of me loves all of you. I am yours.

Confession

Ruach Hakkodesh, be gracious to me according to your lovingkindness. According to the greatness of your compassion, blot out my transgressions. Wash me thoroughly from my iniquity and cleanse me from my sin. For I know my transgressions, and my sin is ever before me. Against you and you only I have sinned and done what is evil in your sight. You are justified when you speak and blameless when you judge.

Thanksgiving

Ruach Hakkodesh, thank you for the closeness of your presence. Thank you for your whispering voice when I'm in danger. Thank you for convicting me of sin before I commit it. Thank you for guiding me with wisdom. Thank you for being the everlasting *Ruach Hakkodesh* and for always being there when I need you the most. My heart gives you the gratitude that comes with knowing how important you truly are to me. Receive the thanksgiving I offer you with pleasure, and may it bring you joy and delight.

Supplication

Lord God, create in me a clean heart and renew a steadfast spirit within me. Do not cast me away from your presence and do not take *Ruach Hakkodesh* from me. Restore to me the joy of your salvation and sustain me with a willing spirit. Then I will teach transgressors your ways, and sinners will be turned to you. Open my lips that my mouth may declare your praise. You do not delight in sacrifice, or I would bring it. You are not pleased with a burnt offering. The sacrifices you desire from me are a broken spirit and a contrite heart. By your favor, do good to me, *Ruach Hakkodesh*.

JEHOVAH SALI

THE LORD MY ROCK

*The LORD is my rock [Jehovah Sali], my fortress
and my deliverer; my God is my rock, in whom I take refuge,
my shield and the horn of my salvation, my stronghold.*

PSALM 18:2 NIV

Adoration

Jehovah Sali, your Word says that when the righteous cry out,
you hear and deliver them. I praise you because you are my rock
when I'm in distress. You are a God of great compassion, mercy,
and grace. Your heart overflows with abundant love—a love that
shields me when I am in need. You are my rock and my fortress,
my strong deliverer. You are high and lifted up on the mountain
of peace. Holy are you, *Jehovah Sali*, as you show your strength to
those in need.

Confession

Jehovah Sali, when I'm in pain or in need, I sometimes turn to
things to distract me—social media, food, a relationship…any-
thing to take my mind off what I'm facing. Forgive me for not
remembering that my deliverance is only a prayer away. Forgive
me for forgetting your name, *Jehovah Sali*, when I am in need.

Thanksgiving

Jehovah Sali, there aren't enough words to thank you adequately for how near your deliverance is to me. It's not just in the big things. You deliver me from destructive thoughts. You deliver me from wasting time by worrying and fretting. You deliver me by reminding me of your names and restoring peace in my heart. Thank you for showing yourself strong day in and day out, for never leaving me or forsaking me, and for always being my shield, my rock, my fortress, and my deliverer.

Supplication

Jehovah Sali, where would I be without you? I would be lost. How could I juggle all the things I try to do without your shield to guard me from the darts of the enemy? I could not. I ask you to stand ready, as you always do, to protect me from dangers I'm not even aware of. Surround me with your angels and cover me with the blood of Jesus Christ as I drive, eat, and go about my day. Dangers lurk all around, and we often lose sight of the most common ones, but you protect me each day. I pray each day to be set on the rock, *Jehovah Sali*, because to step off this rock is to put myself in danger.

JEHOVAH SHALOM

THE LORD OUR PEACE

Gideon built an altar there to the LORD and named it The LORD is Peace [Jehovah Shalom].

JUDGES 6:24

Adoration

Jehovah Shalom, you spoke to the wind and the waves, and you calmed them with just one word. You still the storm within me when I call on your name. You bring peace to my heart and soul when I abide in your presence. In you is the fullness of peace and truth. Regardless of our pedigree, background, education, or status, you choose to raise us up and bring us peace in your name. Just as you delivered Israel through Gideon, you can bring peace to those around me through me when I commit my life to you in all I do. I praise you, for you are the author and finisher of my peace.

Confession

Jehovah Shalom, worry plagues us as a nation. We spend billions of dollars on prescription drugs to help calm our anxiety. Peace is a luxury that large homes and high salaries don't seem to provide. Peace escapes many of us. I admit it escapes me more often than it should. With faith comes peace. With trust comes peace. With rest comes peace. Forgive me for lacking in all three, and give me the grace of your peace.

Thanksgiving

Jehovah Shalom, my heart is filled to overflowing with gratitude for the wonderful peace you offer to me. Fear and anxiety have so many causes today, and many of them are legitimate—trials, dangers, health issues, loss...These things seek to steal my peace. But thank you for being ready and willing to offer this gift of peace to me. Thank you for making your peace available to me if I but ask and believe. Thank you for being my only true peace.

Supplication

Jehovah Shalom, I speak *shalom* into my body—into my cells. I speak *shalom* into my health, calming that which is irritated or aggravated somehow. I speak *shalom* into my mind, my thoughts, and my heart. I call on your name, *Jehovah Shalom*, to be present in all this and more. *Shalom* in my plans, in my future, in my relationships. Show yourself to me and reveal to me the choices I need to make to enter into an even greater level of your peace.

JEHOVAH SHAMMAH

THE LORD IS THERE

*The city shall be 18,000 cubits round about; and
the name of the city from that day shall be, "The
LORD is there" [Jehovah Shammah].*

EZEKIEL 48:35

Adoration

Jehovah Shammah, you live in a place I have never been. You
have established the heavens above me, and they reach far beyond
what I could ever know. My finite mind cannot comprehend you
in all of your majesty, seated there in the new Jerusalem—the place
of your dwelling, the place of *Jehovah Shammah*. Yet you are also
equally here with me right now, and my praise is in your heart and
in your ears. You are my closest friend, and I praise you for all of
your greatness.

Confession

Jehovah Shammah, cause my heart to fully feel the godly sorrow
I should feel when I offend you. You are *Jehovah Shammah*, there
in the place of my eternal home, and yet I dismiss you so easily in
my daily life *here*. Help me know the sorrow tied to the sins I commit against you. Forgive me for sometimes feeling that because you
are *Jehovah Shammah*, you aren't close enough to me to give me the
comfort and love I need as I navigate through this world. Remind
me again and again that you are my *Jehovah Shammah*.

Thanksgiving

Jehovah Shammah, you are high and lofty, and the train of your robe fills the temple of the new Jerusalem. Thank you for preparing a place where we will dwell with you for eternity. I know that though you are there, you are also here. Your eye is on the world, but at the same time your eye is on the lowly sparrow. You surround the universe, but you also surround me. Thank you for being there and for being here in me at the same time.

Supplication

Jehovah Shammah, I ask you to help me know that everything is going to be okay as I go through this day, this month, and this year. The challenges I face are often too much for me to bear. May I call on your name, *Jehovah Shammah*, as a reminder that you have gone before me and are already resting where I will one day be, in your presence and in your place. Let that truth keep me in peace while I go through my daily life. Give me a deeper awareness of your greatness, *Jehovah Shammah*. Give me a glimpse of where you are—*there*.

JEHOVAH TSIDKENU

THE LORD OUR RIGHTEOUSNESS

In His days Judah will be saved,
And Israel will dwell securely;
And this is His name by which He will be called,
"The LORD our righteousness [Jehovah Tsidkenu]."

JEREMIAH 23:6

Adoration

Jehovah Tsidkenu, I have no righteousness of my own that comes from obeying the law, but the righteousness I have comes through faith in Christ. It is the righteousness that depends entirely on faith. Through this faith, you give me a clean slate of purity, bought and earned through the life of Christ. I praise you for your goodness and grace and for the mercies you give me each and every moment of every day. For my sake you made him to be sin who knew no sin so that in him I might become the righteousness of God. Thank you.

Confession

Jehovah Tsidkenu, I come to you with a heart of anguish for all of the sins I have ever committed, seeking your forgiveness and mercy. Forgive me for every unkind word I have ever thought or spoken. Forgive me for every selfish act I have ever committed. Forgive the hardness of my heart and my lack of faith. Pardon my fears, remove my doubts, and cover my insecurities with your righteous, covenantal love.

Thanksgiving

Jehovah Tsidkenu, thank you for imputing your righteousness to me so that I stand in the promises of your covenantal care—not because of anything I have done but because of your great love. Thank you for cleansing me from all unrighteousness and for covering me with the blood of Jesus Christ. This righteousness that I now enjoy came at a great cost to the Son of God, and my heart overflows with gratitude as I think of all you have done for me.

Supplication

Jehovah Tsidkenu, as you cover me in your righteousness, I pray for the grace to be ever mindful of the cost of this gift. I do not want to treat it lightly or dismiss the price you paid to offer this to me. But also, help me to embrace this gift so I can stand tall and confident before you. Keep my heart open to you so that I may approach you and seek the covenant promises you have made to those who stand in the righteousness of Jesus Christ. Make me useful to you as I serve in humility and worship in righteousness before your throne.

IMMANUEL

GOD WITH US

Therefore the Lord Himself will give you a sign:
Behold, a virgin will be with child and bear a
son, and she will call His name Immanuel.

ISAIAH 7:14

Adoration

Immanuel, God with us. The highest, most perfect being—the
Creator of all things—chose to dwell among us. You became a
baby in a barn. You didn't allow your surroundings to define you.
You didn't allow your humanity to limit you. You are fully God but
also fully man, and you took on the sin of all humanity to offer us
salvation. *Immanuel,* there is none like you. You are the hope of
glory. You are the ever-present help in time of need. You are closer
than a brother, dearer than a friend. You are the King of kings, in a
manger—the humble King, who came to reveal the character and
heart of the Father to us all.

Confession

Immanuel, we focus on you a lot during Christmas. We set out
our nativity scenes and hang our stars. We pay attention to you
and give you the honor due you. But so often throughout the rest
of the year, we forget the significance of your name—God with
us, *Immanuel,* God in the flesh. Forgive me for being so easily dis-
tracted that I fail to give you the honor due you every day. Forgive

me for looking outside of you for that which only you can supply—
my meaning, purpose, and life.

Thanksgiving

Immanuel, you humbled yourself and came in the form of a
man so we could see what the Father truly looks like. Thank you
for leaving heaven to come to us on earth. Thank you for showing
us the model of true love, sacrifice, and forgiveness. Thank you for
being my *Immanuel*, my friend, and my Lord. You know what it's
like to be human—to hurt, to be alone. And because you know,
you show me compassion when I am weak. Thank you for your
compassion, *Immanuel*. You are my Savior and King.

Supplication

Immanuel, I pray that people around the world and in our
nation will come to know you as "God with them." I pray your
name will be spread in such a way as to draw people to you.
Strengthen your followers in your kingdom to live lives that reflect
your glory and point people to you as King, as God with us. May
we experience you more fully and intimately each day. May you
not be to us a distant God, far off, but may we know you as *Immanuel*, God with us. May I know you as *Immanuel*, God with me.

GO'EL

KINSMAN REDEEMER

In Your lovingkindness You have led the people
whom You have redeemed [Go'el];
In Your strength You have guided them
to Your holy habitation.

EXODUS 15:13

Adoration

Go'el, it is because of your lovingkindness that we have received your redemption. Your heart is full of kindness and gentleness toward your people. Your thoughts toward me honor me with a love like nothing I have ever known. You esteem me with your grace and redemption, and for that I praise you with all I am. I lift my voice to announce your goodness to all who will hear. I stand with a heart filled to the fullest with a hope that comes from knowing you as my faithful kinsman redeemer. You have bought me with the blood of Jesus Christ and have led me to your holy habitation.

Confession

Go'el, how frequently I underestimate what you have done for me. You have surely redeemed me from the pit and set me on high in the presence of Almighty God, yet I dismiss you in my thoughts or fill my time with things of lesser importance. You are the great and holy God, who lives in a great and holy habitation, and yet I remain in the confines of my own finite weaknesses too often when I cling to my surroundings rather than abide with you in yours. Forgive my selfishness in failing to acknowledge you as *Go'el*, my kinsman redeemer, and everything that entails.

Thanksgiving

Go'el, thank you for seeing me as I was—a sinner unable to redeem myself. Just as Boaz saw Ruth as she gleaned in the field, you have seen me in my helpless state, and you approached me to secure my redemption. You didn't leave me where I was—lost and alone. Because of your great grace, which rescued me from the enemy, I now have hope. Thank you for a new hope that gives me the courage to face each day with confidence in your redemptive power.

Supplication

Go'el, will you walk with me so closely that I can tell you are there? Will you make me aware of your presence? You are my kinsman redeemer, who has delivered me from a life of eternal pain. Help me to experience your redemption every day. Help me discover the fullness of the abundant life that you came to secure and that you now offer me so freely through the redemption of Jesus Christ. Help me know the blessing of your redemption by showing me the beauty of your moment-by-moment grace. I love you, *Go'el*—you are my family. You stick closer to me than a brother.

KADOSH

THE HOLY ONE

*"To whom then will you liken Me
That I would be his equal?" says the Holy One [Kadosh].*

ISAIAH 40:25

Adoration

Kadosh, in the year King Uzziah died, Isaiah saw you seated on a throne, high and lifted up, with the train of your robe filling the temple. Above you he saw seraphim, each having six wings. With two wings they covered their faces, with two wings they covered their feet, and with the remaining two wings they flew. As Isaiah stood there watching, he could hear the voice of one of the seraphim calling out to another one saying, "Holy, holy, holy is the LORD of hosts; the whole earth is full of his glory." Indeed, holy, holy, holy are you, *Kadosh*. The whole earth is full of your glory.

Confession

Kadosh, the foundations of the thresholds shook at the voice of the seraphim as they called out to each other, "Holy, holy, holy is the LORD of hosts, the whole earth is full of his glory." The temple was filling with smoke. The entire scene responded to your holiness. Your intangible holiness affected Isaiah's tangible environment that day. Forgive me for failing to respond to your holiness at the level due you. Forgive me for so easily dismissing the power and purity of who you are. May I respond in total praise and humility as you make me aware of your holiness, my *Kadosh*.

Thanksgiving

Kadosh, thank you for revealing to me the great grace that is mine and that allows me to enter your presence. Just as the angel flew to Isaiah with the coal he had taken from the altar and touched Isaiah's lips with it, you have cleansed me from all unrighteousness through the substitutionary atonement of Jesus Christ in his death, burial, and resurrection. I am unclean, and I live among a people who are unclean, yet you have cleansed me and made me as holy as you are. Thank you for your merciful love, *Kadosh*, which enables me to know you and be accepted by you.

Supplication

Kadosh, let your holiness manifest itself in me. May it transform my speech, my thoughts, and my actions. You have purchased my purity at such a great cost. I do not want it to be wasted in my life. Help me to honor you in all I do. Guide my decisions with the wisdom of your Word. Show me how to live in the fullness of knowing you and make my life a holy instrument acceptable to you, which is my spiritual service of worship. Help me focus on your holiness and not on my past or present sins so I won't become weighed down in guilt and grief. Instead, empower me to live a life set apart to you.

RUACH ELOHIM

SPIRIT OF GOD

*When they came to the hill there, behold, a group of prophets
met him; and the Spirit of God [Ruach Elohim] came
upon him mightily, so that he prophesied among them.*

1 SAMUEL 10:10

Adoration

Ruach Elohim, you are the Spirit of the living God. In you I put
my hope and trust. Because of you I'm able to experience the fullness of God in my life. Freedom comes as you reign in my life. You
guide and direct me in my thoughts. You pray for me with words
I don't even know I need to pray. You are the Spirit of God, his
helper, his mighty breath. I lift you up and honor you. May your
fullness be known to this world, which needs you so desperately.

Confession

Ruach Elohim, please forgive me for the sins I harbor in my
heart. Forgive me for envy. Forgive me when I look at other people's lives that appear to be so picture-perfect that I begin to
become ungrateful for all you have done for me. Forgive me when
I am jealous, comparing your path for me with the favor and grace
you have given to others on their path. That only causes distance
between me and you, and I need to be close to you. I confess these
sins to you and ask you to keep me from them in the future.

Thanksgiving

Ruach Elohim, thank you for your kindness and faithfulness. Thank you for living in me. Thank you for imparting the wisdom of your Word to my heart. Thank you for all of this and even more. Thank you for being with me even when I feel so alone. I may even wonder who cares. But I know you are there, *Ruach Elohim*, and you are near.

Supplication

Ruach Elohim, I bless your name and lift up your holiness to be praised as I ask you to be ever present in my spirit. May your Holy Spirit dominate my own. I don't want to wrestle anymore with fear, pain, or doubt. I want the trust and rest that come from your presence to be evident in all I do and feel. I seek you, *Ruach Elohim*—I seek your closeness to me. I need your presence in all I do—in each day, each moment. Help me know you and love you as I ought.

JEHOVAH MALAKH

THE ANGEL OF THE LORD

Now the angel of the LORD [Jehovah Malakh]
found her by a spring of water in the wilderness,
by the spring on the way to Shur.

GENESIS 16:7

Adoration

Jehovah Malakh, I praise you, for you seek those who are lost. You seek out the lonely with the message of hope. You found Hagar when she had been driven into the wilderness, and you gave her compassion from on high. She thought her life was over, but you showed her that she had a future and a hope. I praise you, for you are the messenger of God, seeking those who need to hear from him the most. May you be praised, *Jehovah Malakh*, with the highest praise.

Confession

Jehovah Malakh, I don't always honor you as I should in my words and thoughts. When I'm alone and fearing for my future, just as Hagar was, I don't always look for you and your message of hope to me. Sometimes I become fearful and try to take measures in my own hands. Forgive me, *Jehovah Malakh*, for failing to give you the glory due your holy name.

Thanksgiving

Jehovah Malakh, thank you for bringing hope to those in need. Thank you for finding me in my darkest and deepest hour of pain, giving me a message from my King. Thank you for your faithfulness to the Father and for caring about me when I've been unwilling or unable to care for myself. You know the path I'm to take, and you know the future I'm to have. Thank you for coming to me when I can't see and for sharing the truth of the Lord my God.

Supplication

Jehovah Malakh, there is power that comes from knowing you and experiencing you. Some things are out of my control—situations in my family, at work, or with my health. Whatever it is, you know all about it. Only you have the power to break through that which surrounds me and to comfort me when I'm in distress. Will you come, *Jehovah Malakh*? I need you near me. I need to hear the message my God has for me. Come and tell me the good things he has for me that I may hope again in him.

JEHOVAH TSEMACH

THE BRANCH OF THE LORD

*In that day the Branch of the LORD [Jehovah Tsemach] will
be beautiful and glorious, and the fruit of the earth will
be the pride and the adornment of the survivors of Israel.*

ISAIAH 4:2

Adoration

Jehovah Tsemach, you are beautiful. You are glorious. The fruit
of the earth is the pride and adornment of all of us who call on your
name. *Jehovah Tsemach*, you are the branch that God has planted,
a branch that cannot and will not be uprooted—the branch of
his planting and purpose. I praise you for the victory you have
achieved and for the life-giving sustenance you provide to all those
who call on your name. May we adorn ourselves with the beauty of
your name and rest in the abundance of your fruit, and may you
teach us to look to you as we offer the fruit of our lips in humble
praise and thanksgiving.

Confession

Jehovah Tsemach, forgive me for the uncleanliness within me.
Look on me with your great compassion, for you know that I am
but dust. My heart wanders quickly from you after things I desire,
or down paths of fear and anxiety. Whatever it is, I have offended
you with my sin, and as a result you have sent your branch, *Jehovah
Tsemach*, who grants me purity in his name. Look on our nation as

well and cleanse us in the power of your name. Purge the blood-shed from among us and grant us refuge from the storm we have brought on our land through our rebellion against your righteous statutes and laws.

Thanksgiving

Jehovah Tsemach, thank you for bringing your holiness and purity to me. Thank you for not leaving me alone to die or to remain in the stain of my own sins. I have hope because of your great love. You have not only cleansed me, *Jehovah Tsemach*, but also sheltered me from the heat of the day. You are my refuge from the ills of this life. My heart overflows with a good theme—it is the sound of gratitude. Receive my thanksgiving, and may it bring you pleasure and delight.

Supplication

Jehovah Tsemach, I praise you for your gracious forgiveness, for you have redeemed me from the pit and cleansed me from all that needed to be washed away. Lord, I also pray that in your power and might you will keep me from that which causes you pain and which ultimately causes me pain as well. Stay ever close to me to watch over me and guide me along the path of wisdom and righteousness so that I may feel your pleasure in all I do. I ask also that you will raise up leaders for our nation who will instruct us according to your kingdom agenda and take us in a new direction of honoring you throughout our land.

ESH OKLAH

CONSUMING FIRE

For the LORD your God is a consuming
fire [Esh Oklah], a jealous God.

DEUTERONOMY 4:24

Adoration

Esh Oklah, you are a consuming fire. You instruct us not to worship any other gods because you are a jealous God. Your emotions are strong, and you tell us time and again in your Word that you will not share your glory with any other. I lift up your name in praise and thanksgiving for your great might, which set the stars in place, and also for your delicate hand, which orders the steps on my path. A consuming God who is larger than the universe but also cares deeply for my affections is a God to be worshipped at all times.

Confession

Esh Oklah, if time were a measurement of my affections, where would you stand? I give so much of my time to entertainment, work, or simple distractions, often just passing the time. Yet you are a jealous God and a consuming fire—a God I should not take lightly. I confess that I often set my heart on things other than you. You know this already, but I want you to know that I know it too, and I humbly ask for you to forgive me. Be gracious to me and draw my heart to you.

Thanksgiving

Esh Oklah, thank you, my God, that though you are a consuming fire, you also show restraint. Thank you for not repaying me as my sins deserve. You have not dealt with me according to my unfaithfulness to you. Thank you for the kindness of your patience and for the intensity of your love. If you didn't truly love me, you wouldn't care where I set my heart. It's precisely because you care about me so deeply that your consuming fire blazes strong when my affections turn to things other than you. Thank you for the passion of your love.

Supplication

Esh Oklah, will you remind me that you are a consuming fire, but will you do it gently with your grace? I don't want to minimize you in my life, but I often do so simply out of neglect. Cultivate in me the finest love toward you that I can have. Cultivate actions that reflect that love, *Esh Oklah*. Draw me to you in total faithfulness so that I may not provoke your jealousy in any way. I want you to be first in my heart, mind, and soul, just as you have instructed me to do. And yet you know that I am mere dust. I ask you to teach and train me to honor you as you are due.

'AB

FATHER

A father ['Ab] of the fatherless and a judge for the widows,
Is God in His holy habitation.

PSALM 68:5

Adoration

'Ab, you are a father to the fatherless and the defender of those
in need. Holy is your name, for you stand above all. I lift up your
name in praise and adoration, acknowledging you as my Father, a
Father who is always there when I need you. Sometimes our earthly
fathers abandon us or don't know how to be there when we need
them. But when that happens, you rise up as our true Father. You
fill the gap and bring comfort and guidance to each of us who seeks
your face as Father. You have so many children, *'Ab*, that I don't
know how you could keep track of us all at one time, but you do.
You are the greatest Father of all

Confession

'Ab, how many times have I neglected to receive the comfort
and care you have for me as my Father because I forget that you
are there? Or because I simply don't know you by this name? You
are God. You are the Creator. You are holy. And sometimes that
makes me feel as if you are also distant. Yet the name *'Ab* tells me
that you are not distant at all. In fact, you are as close to me as a

father is to his child. When I'm afraid, I will trust in you because you hold my cares in your hand. You hold my heart in your own.

Thanksgiving

'Ab, thank you for not leaving me as an orphan. Whether my earthly father is near and dear or is someone I do not know, he can't be everything I need in a father because no human being is perfect. Only you are perfect, and only you provide me with all of the loving, gentle care a daddy can give. Thank you for your patience, kindness, and goodness. Thank you for being merely a breath away. When I whisper your name—'Ab, Father—you hear.

Supplication

'Ab, I want to know you more. I want to experience your presence more. I want to understand what it means to live each day of my life in the fullness of who you are and in the peace that comes from trusting in you as my Father. I want to seek your wisdom in my choices instead of rushing ahead to pursue dead ends. Forgive me for making hasty decisions and show me instead how to look to you as my Father—the one who guides me in every step I take. When I am empty, fill me with your powerful and abiding paternal care.

'OR GOYIM

A LIGHT TO THE NATIONS

I am the LORD, I have called You in righteousness,
I will also hold You by the hand and watch over You,
And I will appoint You as a covenant to the people,
As a light to the nations ['Or Goyim].

ISAIAH 42:6

Adoration

'Or Goyim, you are a light to the nations. You are a covenant to the people. In your righteousness we find our salvation. You are my God, *'Or Goyim*. I praise you, for your salvation reaches to the farthest lands and stretches across all continents. Tribes and tongues of people do not yet know you, but I pray you will send your servants to them to take your love to the lost. You have called the nations your own. You are the King over all. I lift up your name, *'Or Goyim*, and praise you for extending your hand to the nations.

Confession

'Or Goyim, I come to you on behalf of each of us in the body of Christ who has failed to do all that we can to take your name to the nations. You are a light to the nations, but so many people are lost in darkness simply because they haven't heard about you. How will they hear unless someone is sent? Send us, Lord, to those in the world who do not yet know about you. Show us how to take

your name to those in need and give the light of your hope to a dying world.

Thanksgiving

'Or Goyim, you deserve all praise and thanksgiving, for you have brought the fullness of salvation to all nations. Thank you for opening up your goodness and grace to all who trust in you. Thank you for not closing off the gift of your salvation to any nation and for providing the hope of eternity to any who will believe on you. Thank you for redeeming us and drawing us into your light, for in your righteousness we will find our own.

Supplication

'Or Goyim, may your name be great among the nations. May your name be praised around the world. May people from all tongues and tribes lift up your name and seek your face for salvation. Send your kingdom servants to every corner of this world to proclaim the message of the covenantal love Jesus Christ died to provide for those who trust in him in faith. Raise up a generation of those who want nothing more than to proclaim that you are the light of the world to all nations. Make your name known, 'Or Goyim, make your name known.

ABOUT DR. TONY EVANS

Dr. Tony Evans is founder and senior pastor of the 9500-member Oak Cliff Bible Fellowship in Dallas, founder and president of The Urban Alternative, chaplain of the NBA's Dallas Mavericks, and author of *Destiny, Victory in Spiritual Warfare, God's Unlikely Path to Success, The Power of God's Names*, and *A Moment for Your Soul*. His radio broadcast, *The Alternative with Dr. Tony Evans*, can be heard on nearly 1000 US outlets daily and in more than 100 countries.

THE URBAN ALTERNATIVE

Dr. Evans and The Urban Alternative (TUA) equip, empower, and unite Christians to impact *individuals, families, churches,* and *communities* to restore hope and transform lives.

We believe the core cause of the problems we face in our personal lives, homes, churches, and societies is a spiritual one. Therefore, the only way to address them is spiritually. We've tried political, social, economic, and even religious agendas. It's time for a kingdom agenda—God's visible and comprehensive rule over every area of life because when we function as we were designed, God's divine power changes everything. It renews and restores as the life of Christ is made manifest in our own. As we align ourselves under him, he brings about full restoration from deep within. In this atmosphere, people are revived and made whole.

As God's kingdom impacts us, it impacts others—transforming every sphere of life. When each biblical sphere of life functions in accordance with God's Word, the outcomes are evangelism, discipleship, and community impact. As we learn how to govern ourselves under God, we transform the institutions of family, church, and society according to a biblically based kingdom perspective. Through Him, we are touching heaven and changing earth.

To achieve our goal, we use a variety of strategies, methods, and resources for reaching and equipping as many people as possible.

Broadcast Media

Hundreds of thousands of individuals experience *The Alternative with Dr. Tony Evans* through daily radio broadcasts on nearly 1000 radio outlets and in more than 100 countries. The broadcast can also be seen on several television networks and online at TonyEvans.org.

Leadership Training

Kingdom Agenda Pastors (KAP) provides a viable network for like-minded pastors who embrace the kingdom agenda philosophy. Pastors have the opportunity to go deeper with Dr. Evans as they are given greater biblical knowledge, practical applications, and resources to impact individuals, families, churches, and communities. KAP welcomes senior and associate pastors of all churches.

Kingdom Agenda Pastors' Summit progressively develops church leaders to meet the demands of the twenty-first century while maintaining the gospel message and the strategic position of the church. The Summit introduces intensive seminars, workshops, and resources, addressing issues affecting the community, family, leadership, organizational health, and more.

Pastors' Wives Ministry, founded by Dr. Lois Evans, provides counsel, encouragement, and spiritual resources for pastors' wives as they serve with their husbands in the ministry. The ministry focuses on the KAP Summit, which offers senior pastors' wives a safe place to reflect, renew, and relax along with training in personal development, spiritual growth, and care for their emotional and physical well-being.

Community Impact

National Church Adopt-A-School Initiative (NCAASI) prepares churches across the country to impact communities by using public schools as the primary vehicle for effecting positive social change in urban youth and families. Leaders of churches, school districts, faith-based organizations, and other nonprofit organizations are equipped with the knowledge and tools to forge partnerships and build strong social-service delivery systems. This training is based on the comprehensive church-based community impact strategy conducted by Oak Cliff Bible Fellowship. It addresses such areas as economic development, education, housing, health revitalization, family renewal, and racial reconciliation. We also assist churches in tailoring the model to meet the specific needs of their communities while simultaneously addressing the spiritual and moral frame of reference.

Resource Development

We are fostering lifelong learning partnerships with the people we serve by providing a variety of published materials. We offer booklets, Bible studies, books, CDs, and DVDs to strengthen people in their walk with God and ministry to others.

—

For more information, call
(800) 800-3222

or write
The Urban Alternative
PO Box 4000
Dallas, TX 75208

or visit our website at
TonyEvans.org

More excellent books from Dr. Tony Evans and Harvest House Publishers

Victory in Spiritual Warfare

In this timely, unique exploration of spiritual warfare, Dr. Evans unveils a simple yet radical truth: Every struggle and conflict in the physical realm has its root in the spiritual realm. With passion and clarity, Dr. Evans demystifies spiritual warfare so you can tackle challenges and obstacles with spiritual power—God's authority—as you...

- understand how the battle is fought by Satan
- actively use the armor of God
- find strength in prayer and sufficiency in Christ
- win over chemical, sexual, emotional, relational, and other strongholds

Dr. Evans is compelling, down-to-earth, and excited for believers to experience their victory in Christ and embrace the life, hope, and purpose God has for them.

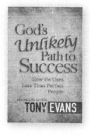

God's Unlikely Path to Success

When many Christian readers think of the heroes of the Bible, they think about how "good" they were. They forget that....

Rahab was a harlot.
Jonah was a rebel.
Moses was a murderer.
Sarah was a doubter.
Peter was an apostate.
Esther was a diva.
Samson was a player.
Jacob was a deceiver.

And yet these eight men and women are among the Bible's greatest heroes. Dr. Evans uses these prominent Bible characters to illustrate the truth that God delights in using imperfect people who have failed, sinned, or just plain blown it. These are men and women whose actions were not consistent with God's character, and yet God met them and used them in the midst of their mess.

You will be encouraged about your own walk with God as you come to understand that he has you, too, on a path to success, despite your imperfections and mistakes.

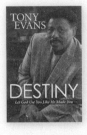

Destiny

God has ordained a custom-designed life for you that leads to the expansion of his kingdom. Until you discover the reason why you were uniquely created, you will be empty and frustrated. But a clear understanding of your personal assignment from God brings about your deepest satisfaction, God's greatest glory, and the greatest benefit to others. You'll embark on a journey to discover your particular calling—a journey that includes...

- affirming God's plan to give you a unique destiny
- using practical tools to identify your special assignment from God
- growing into the fullness of your destiny

Understanding God's kingdom agenda for the whole world and his singular role for you leads to a future that is bright with hope.

A Moment for Your Soul

In this uplifting devotional, Dr. Evans offers a daily reading for Monday through Friday and one for the weekend—all compact, powerful, and designed to reach your deepest need. Each entry includes a relevant Scripture reading for the day.

This daily touchstone for growing Christians is easy to tuck into your purse or briefcase as a constant companion and will make the perfect gift for any special occasion.

The Power of God's Names

Dr. Tony Evans shows that God reveals his nature to us through his names. Who is God in his fullness? How has he expressed his riches and righteousness? How can you trust his goodness? As you get to know the names of God and understand their meaning, God's character will become real to you in life-changing ways. You will explore the depths of God as...

Elohim—the All-Powerful Creator
Jehovah—the Self-Revealing One
Adonai—the Owner of All
Jehovah Jireh—the Lord Who Provides
El Shaddai—the Almighty Sufficient One
El Elion—the Most High Ruler
Jehovah Nissi—the Lord's Banner of Victory
Jehovah Shalom—the Lord Our Peace
Jehovah Mekadesh—the Lord Who Sanctifies
Jehovah Rophe—the Lord Who Heals
Jehovah Tsidkenu—the Lord My Righteousness
Jehovah Robi—the Lord My Shepherd
Immanuel—God with Us

By studying and understanding the characteristics of God as revealed through his names, you will be better equipped to face hardship and victory, loss and provision, and all of the challenges life throws at you.

To learn more about Harvest House books and
to read sample chapters, visit our website:

www.harvesthousepublishers.com

HARVEST HOUSE PUBLISHERS
EUGENE, OREGON